how to talk to yourself

how to talk to yourself

From Self-Doubt to Self-Confidence

Ro Mitchell

BLUEBIRD

First published 2025 by Bluebird
an imprint of Pan Macmillan
The Smithson, 6 Briset Street, London EC1M 5NR
EU representative: Macmillan Publishers Ireland Ltd, 1st Floor,
The Liffey Trust Centre, 117–126 Sheriff Street Upper,
Dublin 1 D01 YC43
Associated companies throughout the world

ISBN 978-1-0350-6044-3

Copyright © Ro Mitchell 2025

The right of Ro Mitchell to be identified as the
author of this work has been asserted in accordance
with the Copyright, Designs and Patents Act 1988.

All rights reserved. No part of this publication may be reproduced,
stored in a retrieval system, or transmitted, in any form, or by any means
(including, without limitation, electronic, mechanical, photocopying,
recording or otherwise) without the prior written permission of the publisher.

Pan Macmillan does not have any control over, or any responsibility for,
any author or third-party websites (including, without limitation, URLs,
emails and QR codes) referred to in or on this book.

1 3 5 7 9 8 6 4 2

A CIP catalogue record for this book is available from the British Library.

Typeset in Palatino by Palimpsest Book Production Ltd, Falkirk, Stirlingshire
Printed and bound by CPI Group (UK) Ltd, Croydon, CR0 4YY

This book is sold subject to the condition that it shall not, by way of
trade or otherwise, be lent, hired out, or otherwise circulated without
the publisher's prior consent in any form of binding or cover other than
that in which it is published and without a similar condition including this
condition being imposed on the subsequent purchaser. The publisher does not
authorize the use or reproduction of any part of this book in any manner for the
purpose of training artificial intelligence technologies or systems. The publisher
expressly reserves this book from the Text and Data Mining exception in accordance
with Article 4(3) of the European Union Digital Single Market Directive 2019/790.

Visit **www.panmacmillan.com/bluebird** to read more
about all our books and to buy them.

For Sunny

This book contains potentially triggering themes of eating disorders, body image and body dysmorphia, bullying, descriptions of anxiety attacks and descriptions of depression. All names, locations and dates have been changed to protect the privacy of individuals.

Contents

	Introduction	1

Part 1: Listen to Yourself   7

1	Confronting Negative Self-talk	11
2	Unfriending Your Inner Critic	33
3	The Comparison Trap	47
4	Insecurity Is Lonely	61

Part 2: Talk to Yourself   73

5	Unlearning Shame	75
6	Proactive Changes	103
7	Talking Back	121
8	Making Acceptance Second Nature	131

Part 3: Forgive Yourself   145

9	Hurt People Hurt People	149
10	Humans Make Mistakes	163
11	You Deserve Good Things	175

Part 4: Be Kind to Yourself 185

12	Fundamental Health	187
13	Maintain	201
14	Protect	217
15	Who Are You?	229

Afterword 239
Acknowledgements 241

Introduction

Sand slips like water through my fingers as I trace my hands through the grains around me, patterns fading as quickly as they form. The beach is calm and quiet, only the gentle lapping of waves against rocks breaks the silence. My eyes are fixed on the infinite skyline in the evening light, pink and purple and stretching out far beyond the sea. I am both overwhelmed and comforted by its vastness, by how the Earth seems never-ending. By how huge it all is and how small I am. By how your world can feel like it's ending but at the same time, somewhere else, the sea is still the sea, the sky is still the sky, and life continues as it always has. On days when anxiety has squeezed the air from my lungs, and in mornings that followed nights I wasn't sure I would get through, the sun has still risen and the birds have still sung. Nature's indifference comforts me. Its persistence is a constant.

Brushing my hair from my face, I giggle as I watch my dog, Bea, fervently digging up patches of sand, forming a hole that her head momentarily disappears down into. Her nose is caked with sand when she comes up for air, pink tongue lolling as she pants. She digs as though she is nearing hidden treasure, her tail wagging at such intense speed, small paws firing back sand that we'll find in her golden fur for weeks. There is nobody here but us. It feels, for a moment, as though nobody even knows this beach exists. And at this hour, when the road that runs parallel to the beach is deserted, I could trick myself into believing there is nobody else on the planet.

I remember carefree summers spent splashing about in the sea and enjoying picnics on this beach. I used to be jealous of the other kids at school whose holiday destinations were guaranteed to be warm, with water slides and pools and palm trees. Through adult eyes, however, in all its beauty and tranquillity, I'd choose Donegal every time.

I glance down at my legs that I now feel entirely neutral towards, though they have changed so much over the years. A breeze rustles the long grass of the dunes and goosebumps freckle my skin, my shorts and t-shirt not offering much warmth. We should head back soon. When I call her name, Bea bounces towards me, leaving a trail of paw prints in the sand as she runs. She is an image of uninhibited joy. A dog on a beach with no worries, happy just to exist. I feel her joy, so deeply that I can't figure out if I want to laugh or cry, or both. Though overwhelming, I let myself embrace this feeling, a shared happiness washing over me in a wave of nostalgia and clarity. A single tear runs down my cheek and I let it go, warm and wet as it slips under my chin and is absorbed by my collar.

I laugh and more tears trickle down my face. Bea presses her nose into my cheek, ever curious, attuned to my emotion. 'I don't know why I'm crying!' I say to her.

I didn't mean to sit and cry. But what I do know is that these are happy tears. That I am crying because I feel *okay*. Because I feel content. I am alive and grateful. Present. These are tears of realization and remembrance. After a lifetime of mental anguish, it is not lost on me what a privilege it is to feel *okay*. I am crying because I am at peace. What a wonderful thing.

Five years ago, when I walked along this same beach, I was a memory of myself. The mental images I have from that time are blurred: sand but no sky, eyes fixed to the ground, tangled up in worry, living deep within my own mind. The happy, excitable girl I had been in childhood was nowhere to be found. She had been swallowed by this self-loathing version of me, one who was ashamed of her own existence. It was too painful to live in the moment. Haunted by self-hatred, seventeen-year-old me wanted nothing more than to hide from the world. Five years ago, I was living under the rule of an unwell mind. I spent every waking moment tormented by my own thoughts. My focus was only on my body, my weight, and the desolation that consumed me. There was little room to think of anything positive, let alone see all of the beauty surrounding me.

Back then, I saw no way out. I couldn't imagine a life not shrouded in guilt and shame. Less than a month after I last walked along this beach, I gave up on myself completely. I had lost so much to self-doubt, had so much stripped from me because I didn't know how to be kind to myself, how to talk to myself as a friend.

Despite seeing no future for myself, believing I was immune to happiness, here I am. Back on the beach. Happy. Content. Alive. And glad about it. Accepting of my body, thankful for the fight it put up when I was trying so hard to break it down. Accepting of the parts of me that I used to hide away, the parts I used to hate, and of my past.

I'm crying for the version of me who didn't see a future. Because if that version of me could see me now, she'd be crying too. There was hope for me, even if I couldn't see it.

If you are in that place right now, carrying the weight of hopelessness, afraid of the future, I want you to know it's going to be okay. It's okay to feel scared. It's okay if you can't hold the hope for yourself right now. But I know that there is hope for you, just as there was for me. There is a version of you who will look back on the time you're living through now and be so glad you didn't give up. There is a version of you who feels the happiness that you longed for and, most of all, is so proud of how far you have come.

As the soft sunset fades into an early evening darkness, I wander back up the beach, taking a moment to stand in the shallow water, ice-cold as it rises to cover my feet and retreats again.

A mirror cannot reflect back at you the reasons why you are loved.

Part 1
Listen to Yourself

Your journey towards healing, and what has led you to pick up this book, is entirely personal.

You are shaped by your individual experiences, as I am, and as we all are. *How to Talk to Yourself* is a book for you. It is here to be used in the way that you find most helpful. This is a gentle guide towards a positive relationship with yourself, a space to feel understood and to better understand yourself. I'm here to take you through the process step by step, to help you build your confidence, strengthen relationships in your life and understand your self-talk.

For now, all you really need is this book and an open mind, but as there will be exercises to take part in along the way, it may help to have a journal/paper and pen near to hand. There is no pressure; you can dip in and out of these pages, put this book down and take a break whenever you feel you need to. Whether it takes you a day or a year to read these chapters, as long as you learn to be kinder to yourself in the process, my work is done.

This book is about *you*, not me, and while I toyed with whether or not to mention my own mental health history, I feel it's important to acknowledge that, as a teenager, I was unwell, specifically with anorexia. I bring this up as a symbol of hope; to let anyone who is living with mental illness, or who is feeling isolated, stuck and hopeless, know that there is a life for you beyond it. Anorexia, for me, served as a coping mechanism for my low self-esteem and incapacitating anxiety. It was a plaster on a wound. In many ways, I view my eating disorder as a physical manifestation of the unhappiness I had within myself throughout my childhood years. Negative self-talk was a natural extension of that. Though I will refer back to my experience of life with an eating disorder throughout this book, I am not going to delve into the minutiae of it, because at the core of its development was the way in which I spoke to myself, and the greatest aid in my healing from it was self-empowerment. My eating disorder served as a distraction, but negative self-talk is in no way exclusive to eating-disorder sufferers, or people suffering from mental illness. The way we all speak to ourselves matters, however that looks for you. This is a book for everyone.

This is the book that I needed but didn't have during the years I struggled immensely with my mental health. Though the doctors who treated me put little focus on self-talk, changing the way that I spoke to myself was what shaped my recovery journey. Through nurturing a positive relationship with myself, and learning to flip the narrative I had built over many years, I have created a life I am now content in. And though I am so grateful for the external support I received; I know that healing comes from within. It wouldn't have happened without the persistent hard work that I put in. After four years of practice, trial and error, slip-ups and strides forward, I have found strength within myself and mastered my self-talk. I left behind a girl haunted by self-hatred and anxiety, who was living in a cycle of shame and self-inflicted punishment, and I have come into my own as a confident, present and self-accepting person.

I am writing this book because I have been to the depths of myself, I have grappled with things I thought I'd never survive, and I have come out the other side. I know how it feels to truly believe you'll never like yourself. I know self-critical thought processes inside out. My intricate understanding of them is what I used to build a path towards healing. I am not a doctor, but I am living proof that things can change. Nobody truly understands what it's like to live in that mental space unless they've been through it. I took my happiness into my own hands. I want this book to be a friend, a warm hug, someone to hold you through this journey and show you that, no matter what, you can find the happiness that you so deserve.

I truly believe that when a person can be kind to themselves, life becomes less daunting. Challenges that may have once felt insurmountable become mountains that you can confidently climb. Self-compassion is power.

To embark on a journey towards healing, you must first be aware of what you are healing from. I imagine that many people who have picked up this book have some awareness of the unkind ways in which they talk to themselves, but if you don't, Part 1 will teach you how to differentiate your critical inner voice from the real you. Noticing and strengthening your understanding of negative self-talk is vital. In the coming chapters, we are going to work on becoming alert to the sly ways in which negative self-talk can infiltrate your life, understanding the purpose that it serves, tackling habitual comparison and facing the interpersonal struggles that insecurity can result in.

Chapter 1

Confronting Negative Self-talk

The art of noticing is the first step; change comes after.

'Can you tell me one thing that you like about yourself?'

The air in the room was heavy and stagnant, thick in my throat as I shifted in my chair. I glanced at the clock, at the door, and back to my therapist. She had a gentle expression, warm eyes. She was not too pushy but not disinterested either. I liked her.

She was the fifth therapist to ask me this, though. Having spent years trying various forms of therapy, all of which set out to improve my self-esteem, this is one question that I could always guarantee I'd be asked. I understood the sentiment, but they couldn't get an honest answer out of me – there was no honest answer.

I was an expert in uncomfortable-question evasion, so I simply filled the silence with what she wanted to hear.

Though I held a deep hatred for this question – because, *duh, that's why I'm here, I hate myself* – there was one trait that I would write down time and time again, one quality that I always felt quietly confident in.

I met her eyes for a second. 'Um, I'm kind.'

I am kind. And six years later, I still believe this to be true. I know I have a big heart and I like to think that I'm a kind person – this just isn't a kindness that naturally extends to myself.

For as long as I can remember, my brain has defaulted to negative self-talk. I've always found it much more comfortable to criticize myself, my work, my actions and my appearance than to pay myself a compliment, or cut myself some slack. Even at a very young age, the thoughts that circled my mind were self-critical, unforgiving and most definitely contributed to a chronic lack of self-esteem. It is only since becoming an adult and embarking on my healing journey that I have started to explore exactly why I learned to speak to myself this way, and why so many others do so, just like me.

I assumed that this was just how my brain was wired. I wasn't even aware of the concept of 'being kind to yourself'. A firm believer in treating others the way you want to be treated, my negative self-talk felt contradictory. Yes, I wanted to be treated kindly by those around me, but I didn't understand how to treat myself that way.

We grow up in a world that always wants *more*. Through outdated beliefs ingrained in caregivers, wider society and pushed by the media, we are taught that we need to be the best version of ourselves, in eternal competition not just with those around us, but with our previous achievements. *Do better! Work harder! Stop being lazy! Go, go, go!* To become the ultimate version of ourselves, we must constantly assess where we are failing, what we are doing 'wrong', then make changes to be *more* successful, *more* likeable, a *better* person. We must be harsh and honest with ourselves. We are never just *enough*.

I spent almost all of my teen years following this method. Year after year spent desperately trying to improve myself. I've done it all: the yelling at myself, the calling myself names, berating and insulting not just the vessel that carried me but the traits that made up my personality, too, in a trivial attempt to become the 'perfect person'. It's exhausting. I thought I wasn't cut out for life. I bullied myself so much that I became completely entrenched in a life-threatening eating disorder, which, unsurprisingly, destroyed any hope of achieving the ideal that I was striving for. At just fifteen, I was so insecure in myself and my body that I put all of my focus into shrinking it. So clouded was I by my obsession, I wasn't noticing that every time I got smaller, my life did too.

Human brains can be black and white at times. When I stripped my individual thoughts back to a basic form, they were effectively: *I hate [X] about myself.* And the solution was: *I will do [insert uncomfortable, unenjoyable task here] to fix it.* I did things that I felt were wrong, like eating more than usual one day, and I met that with a punishment, like eating less than normal the next day, to compensate.

Many of the behaviours I engaged in during my teenage years were a form of punishment for perfectly normal, human things. I was steadfast in my belief that I was awful, lazy and useless – a person who *deserved* to suffer. Nothing is sadder than the fact that so many of us live our lives this way, stuck in a hate-filled game of whack-a-mole, striking ourselves down as we try to grow. Though, thankfully, not everybody has experienced such harsh and unforgiving self-talk, for those who do, it is debilitating.

One thing I've learned through my journey to self-acceptance is this: if you don't address the way in which you talk to yourself, it can end up making you sick.

Sat in a hospital bed one night, four years deep into denial that I had an issue, I floated above my body. The room around me softened and slipped away. Beyond monitors and wires, I saw a girl, childlike and afraid, curled tightly in a ball. I didn't recognize her. Though she mirrored all of my features, hers were sunken, sad, her lips chapped and eyes hollow. I'd laughed in the face of the people who'd told me this was how I looked – *unwell* – and though I didn't recognize this version of myself, I knew that girl was me. A version of *me* I'd never seen before, but the version that everyone else had been seeing for years. I saw a version of me who was fighting to stay alive. I saw a version of me I'd refused to look in the eye. She was a shell of herself; beaten down by years of self-punishment, simply existing and hating herself for it. This sudden awakening knocked me like a punch to the stomach. I'd never been so lost.

I wanted to cry, to say how sorry I was, to give her a hug. I wanted to apologize to my body for all that I'd put it through. I looked away from that version of me, guilt twisting in my gut, and I noticed there was somebody standing beside her. Wrapped in a warm glow, a figment of my imagination and yet so tangible, was the Ro I desperately longed to be. She was bright, glimmering, strong, healthy, happy. She lived a life I was desperate for. It was obvious; the very thing that stood between these two versions of me was the thing I'd trusted to make me happier. I'd fallen deep into the self-hatred trap, believing it would lead me to a happier, better self. But this Ro wasn't yelling at herself; she had a mind filled with ideas, plans, memories – beautiful thoughts taking priority over any obsession with how her body looked. She wasn't consumed with baseless guilt. She wasn't a self-improvement project. Most of all, she wasn't afraid.

She was free. *I* wanted to be free.

I turned back to the girl in the hospital bed, for the first time noticing a tiny ember of hope inside her, flickering gently, begging to be seen. And I knew, in that moment, that I wasn't lost. I was far from the glowing girl standing beside me, but I had an ember, and that ember was enough.

As I came back to my body, the fog lifted. I wasn't built this way. I didn't have to spend every waking moment screaming at myself. I didn't have to be controlled. I wanted to be me again. The thoughts weren't me. And this time, when I heard the unmistakable voice of my self-hatred, I knew it was a tangible thing that I could fight.

Of course I'd never managed to find happiness through self-criticism, how could I ever be content when the brain that I spent all my time in was so negative? I'd been going about my pursuit of self-acceptance in all the wrong ways. I left no room to feel the joy I had been desperate for – I had searched for contentment high and low, in every corner of my life, failing to see the power of being kind to myself, failing to realize that I'd struggle to feel happiness if I didn't really believe I deserved to.

Where does it come from, this incessant need to criticize our every move? I'm certain that, for me, it links to the fact that in childhood I had a lack of exposure to self-compassion, as many of us did. I cannot recall a single instance in my early years where a person around me said, 'I am proud of myself'.

To compliment yourself, in my eyes, took guts – no classmates recognized their own intelligence, no friends complimented their own appearance, none of my peers even seemed to admit they were 'good' at anything. To do so would have seemed boastful, and so, at least in my life, the go-to was usually to insult ourselves. Those insults served not to receive a compliment from our peers, but to avoid being labelled as arrogant by them.

I remember others' judgement of any woman who seemed to like herself a little too much, and perhaps this is why no women in my life ever said, 'I feel beautiful', but instead, 'I am so wrinkly', or 'I look fat', or 'I'm so stupid'. If they had spoken positively of themselves, I'm sure they would have been viewed as vain. And that, in part, is what has bred this culture of putting ourselves down. So many of us fear coming across as 'cocky', and in our external efforts to avoid seeming *up ourselves*, our internal monologue begins to echo those fears of appearing arrogant, kick-starting a lifetime of internalized shame around feeling good about ourselves.

It took many years for me to realize I wasn't a terrible person. The thoughts in my head were, in fact, nothing more than thoughts. They weren't facts. The constant onslaught of perfectly curated insults wasn't coming from the real me, but was a manifestation of my learned self-loathing, a separate voice entirely. There was nothing constructive about the criticism I gave myself, it wasn't improving my life. The idea of needing to achieve perfection to be worthy of love and respect is a trap. I learnt the hard way that the goalposts are always going to move. For people like me – perfectionists – this desperation for an unattainable life is draining. You will lose the weight you wanted to, and you will still dislike your body. You will get that job you were desperate for, then compare yourself to those in roles above you, wondering why you're not good enough for that promotion. You'll try everything to force yourself to fit into a perfect little person-shaped mould, and it'll still never feel like enough. Perfection simply cannot be attained, and we will forever be left feeling unworthy. And so this negative-self-talk spiral continues.

I'm going to reference self-talk a lot in this book, if you couldn't already tell. So, for anyone new to the idea of self-talk, or for anyone who finds the whole thing a bit confusing, let's unravel it.

What is self-talk?

Self-talk, in its most basic, neutral form, is the voice in your head. It defines the way in which we talk to ourselves. It draws from the bank of beliefs that we hold about ourselves and the world around us. Self-talk voices our opinions on the fundamentals of us – our mistakes, our passions, our bodies, our appearance, our relationships.

There are many reasons why we might fall into a habit of negative self-talk, but we need to remember that self-talk can also be a real force for good and a friend to empower us if we can learn to talk to ourselves in a way that builds us up rather than tears us down.

Self-talk isn't just our inner voice but also how we talk about ourselves to others – for example, putting ourselves down, expressing pride for our achievements, or rejecting a compliment – and it holds a lot of power over how we feel. Where positive self-talk can make us feel capable, confident and strong, negative self-talk can cause us to feel guilt, be irrationally angry at ourselves and to form insecurities.

I was entrenched in negative self-talk, imprisoned by hyper-fixation on the smallest of flaws, incapable of seeing a bigger picture. I spent my waking hours insulting myself, comparing myself to others and feeling utterly deflated; as I fell asleep each night, I'd dread the next morning when the cycle would start again. With the knowledge that I have now, I feel an urge to hold the face of the girl I was in my hands and yell 'It doesn't matter! It's all irrelevant! Live your life, you are the only person who cares!' But I didn't need that advice then, I just needed compassion.

It wasn't my fault that I couldn't let go, couldn't see past my own negative beliefs, couldn't let joy in, couldn't see the good in myself. The world around me sold self-destruction in a box labelled 'self-improvement'. The way I'd been feeling was normalized. My low self-esteem had been feeding on ideals formed by a society steeped in rigid beauty standards and restrictive norms, growing stronger day by day until it felt empowered enough to take the form of this nasty, berating voice, picking me apart for things I couldn't change. It had long become its own entity, a mindset that I had no control over.

If you are feeling this way too, let me reassure you – there is a life waiting for you outside of this headspace. You do not have to be stuck in the negative self-talk trap, and I hope this book can be your guide out of that space; it just takes a little time, self-compassion and patience.

As a teen in therapy, I had a lot of people tell me that I had an illness in control of me. I cringed every time I heard this.

What do you mean it's not me? It's literally my brain. On reflection, I didn't want to separate myself from my thoughts. It felt like giving up control. When you're stuck inside your own head, it's hard to find separation between the thoughts that you have control over and the thoughts that have control over you.

The night I'd left my body in the hospital, I tuned in. Fighting sleep, I dragged myself to the bathroom, setting my toothbrush on the ledge beneath the mirror. I met my own gaze, eyes heavy with exhaustion, and as my brain processed my reflection, I *heard* those thoughts. They weren't thoughts I hadn't had before, but for the first time in my life I could recognize them as their own entity – a voice distinct from my own. It was deafening and silent, firing a barrage of insults that nobody could hear but me. The hatred I held for myself had taken on the form of something bigger than my inner monologue, something more autonomous than just an opinion of myself, something that felt concrete and real and undeniable. I didn't know how to give myself grace anymore. I had become convinced that others were thinking the same things, that this was not just an opinion, but fact. I didn't feel deserving of kindness. My inner monologue had turned on me and there was a constant cacophony in my head. It was painful to exist. I knew then that I had to fight it.

Having watched what should have been my happiest moments be overshadowed by my lack of self-esteem, I felt angry that I'd been unable to separate myself from those thoughts, as though I was lacking strength. Again, berating myself for failing. Because I hadn't fought back, I felt I'd wasted precious time. That wasn't true at all. The truth was, I didn't know then that was what I needed. I hadn't learned to listen out for overly critical thoughts. I hadn't been shown how to be kind to myself, how to talk to myself positively.

I know some might call me 'crazy' if I told them that I have a little voice in my head. Insane, even, when I explain that I had to learn to talk to myself in order to get better. And I get it; if you're not familiar with the concept of self-talk it can feel absurd, but the truth is that we all live with an inner monologue.

Whether negative self-talk plays a big part in our daily lives or not, we all have the inner critic that you'll hear me reference throughout this book. It's an important part of the human psyche, meant to keep us safe from social disapproval, and to help us learn from our mistakes. For some, it sits quietly, unassuming, unintrusive, rarely unkind. It serves its purpose, it knows when it's needed. For others, the inner critic lives on high alert, poised for attack, and though its purpose is the same – to help us better ourselves – it doesn't quite understand when to stop. It can rage, throw tantrums and scream hell and highwater at the slightest mistake made. It's the voice that tells you you're a selfish failure because you forgot to text your aunt happy birthday. It's the voice that makes you change your outfit three times before you feel okay about how your body looks. It's the voice that replays your most embarrassing moments as you fall asleep.

This is not to say I hear voices that others don't. In fact, I've come to learn that the little voice inside my head isn't anything unusual. Many of us are plagued by a hateful inner monologue, tolerating a torrent of abuse from a voice that we can't escape but that we can change. We may think these thoughts are who we are, and unknowingly, they can seep into our wider lives, putting up barriers in relationships and affecting our health, our work and our happiness.

We all have it, we just experience it at different intensities.

Recognizing the voice in your head

You may not be familiar with the sound of your inner monologue. Throughout this journey, learning to listen to it without judgement will be an important step towards understanding the origins of any negativity.

If you can, find a space to sit in silence for a moment. If you have a mirror close by, it might be helpful to look into it, too. I found that my negative self-talk was loudest when I was faced with my own reflection. If you struggle to identify the voice of your inner critic, it can be useful to begin by noticing any appearance-specific thoughts that come to the surface. Take a second to be with yourself.

Be still, be silent – try to connect with your inner monologue. Notice where your mind goes. Notice any voice or narrative. Where does your mind jump to? Is it a negative space? Is it neutral? Is your internal voice loud or is it quite quiet? Does sitting with yourself, looking at your reflection, taking yourself in, feel comfortable? Or does it instead feel quite difficult?

All you have to do right now is notice. You don't have to do this for long, this is just an exercise to try to help you to recognize the sound of your inner monologue, to allow you to listen to yourself.

I'm guessing, as you've picked up this book, that voice might be louder than you'd like. Perhaps you're familiar with the idea of self-talk and you know you want to change. Perhaps you're only now really noticing that you, too, aren't very kind to yourself. Or maybe you're just curious.

No matter the place you're in, it's my personal belief that we should all be intentional in the way we speak to ourselves. Considering we are the only person we spend every second of every day with, we drastically overlook the need to create a nurturing relationship with ourselves.

At first, the concept of having a relationship with yourself can sound a bit bizarre. *How can I have a relationship with me when I am me?* – but we all have an inner monologue, we all form personal judgements, and the way we speak to ourselves forms the way we experience the world around us. It also has a huge impact on our happiness.

There was a point in my life where all I could hear was the pure hatred, the endless negative self-talk, that my brain threw at me. I see now that it was a huge contributor to my unhappiness. I hated myself for the spots on my skin, for the tiny, human mistakes I made, and God forbid my jeans ever felt a little tighter – that was a chasm of self-hatred I thought I'd be freefalling in forever.

I no longer live in that space. I can sit comfortably in my skin and know that I am doing just fine. My mistakes don't define me. My appearance is the least-interesting part of who I am. I've learned to do the most foreign thing of all – to stand up for myself. To be my own advocate. To champion the good in myself, and to stop dulling myself down in the pursuit of perfection.

I want that for you, too. I want us all to see the good in who we are because it is there, no matter how hard we try to ignore it. We are far too hard on ourselves, and we are deserving of so much more credit than we give.

Self-appreciation is a unique kind of joy, one that allows us to live with our eyes open, to focus on the beauty around us rather than flaws within us. It's self-acceptance that brings the sense of contentment that so many of us search for but do not realize we hold the power to unlock. Being at peace with ourselves opens up space to live in the now, to be present and indulge in the wonders of life happening around us, to live less in our heads. To me, living outside of my own worries means living mindfully, fully.

When we step beyond constant negativity, we create room for positivity to flow in. How could that ever be bad? We are taught to be kind, so why do we deny ourselves that favour?

For those of us with an inner monologue fixed on high alert, fluent in hyper-anxious, hateful self-talk, our inner critic can start to wreak havoc if we don't learn to talk back. It can prevent us accessing opportunities we are capable of, as our lack of self-belief tells us we'll never succeed. It can cause issues in relationships because we can, unintentionally, project our insecurities onto those we love.

The way we talk to ourselves seeps into every corner of our lives. It can be the difference between going for that job you dream of or deciding not to apply because you assume you're not good enough. It can mean isolating from friends because you convince yourself they don't really like you, or it can mean flourishing in friendships with the confidence that if they didn't enjoy spending time with you, they wouldn't.

We can't control much in life, but we do have the power to change our perceptions and reactions. Your perspective of yourself is the lens through which you see the world. This book is your guide to befriending, forgiving and nurturing *you*. Don't underestimate the power in how you talk to yourself; watch how your self-confidence grows when you begin to treat yourself with kindness and respect.

Of all the things that I tried to help me get out of the anguish I was in, changing the way I spoke to myself caused the biggest shift. Looking in the mirror and not experiencing a rush of negative thoughts immediately altered the headspace with which I stepped into my day. I have more space for friends, more energy for the things I love and more love for the things I'd once lost my passion for.

Engaging in positive self-talk showed me that my unhappiness wasn't rooted in my physical 'flaws', but instead in the obsession I had with fixing them. As a long-term acne sufferer, my skin has been a big point of contention for this little voice in my brain. In this case, my negative self-talk actually cost me a substantial amount of money. Week after week, I was trialling new products, watching them break me out, feeling awful and ugly. And the cycle continued. The deliveries of new skincare products I'd ordered in my desperate bid to attain clear skin were racking up, and all the while I was distressing my poor skin, throwing every chemical that claimed it would help at it, irritating it further. The more obsessed with 'fixing' my skin I got, the more miserable I became. Lots of people suffer from acne, and I never look at them and think they're ugly. So why did I find it so upsetting to look at myself when my skin was at its worst? Because, at that time, I hadn't trained my brain to be at peace with myself. When things went wrong, alarm bells sounded. I was constantly firefighting issues within myself that wouldn't have existed had my negative self-talk not told me they did. My entire self-worth was based on my appearance – the perfect target for a hateful brain.

I could hear it in every part of the way I talked to myself. It greeted me as soon as I woke – *I'm lazy, I'm ugly, my skin is gross, I'm so loud and annoying, my face is chubby, my hair looks so bad today, nobody really likes me, I'm going nowhere in life*. That self-talk buzzed around my brain all day, it sat heavy on my chest as I fell asleep. It showed no signs of leaving me be.

In my own healing journey, I decided that facing the voice of my self-loathing head on was the only way forward.

My inner monologue wasn't informed by my own opinions or beliefs. My teenage years were spent in fear of what others thought of me, desperate to avoid the humiliation of looking or behaving even slightly differently from my peers as a teenage girl. I look back now and it makes so much sense as to why I developed a restrictive-eating disorder. No wonder I wanted nothing more than to quietly fade away, to be so small that nobody even noticed me. To be noticed was to be judged, and there were far too many things to keep a handle on to have *any* hope of executing them all perfectly. I couldn't keep up with the task of being a teenage girl. My anorexia allowed me to stop having to; I knew my focus, I knew my goal, I knew that as long as I was limiting what I ate and watching the number on the scale drop, I was doing something right.

Three years into my recovery, I realized that all of the pressure I felt was self-made. That actually I'd spent most of my life not building myself up to become a person I was proud of. Instead, I'd been contorting and moulding the parts of myself that I felt could be one of the reasons why I was seen as ugly or unloveable, into the shape of what I'd learned was the way I should be. But to force myself to be a person I 'thought I should be' was to live behind a mask.

Attempting to live as anybody but your authentic self is very mentally taxing, though many of us don't realize that until we finally stop doing it.

It didn't matter to anyone in my life if my eyebrows looked even. My best friend loved me just as much when I had raging acne on my chin. My parents wanted a happy and healthy daughter, and our relationship improved tenfold when I finally allowed myself to be just that. Everything in my life improved when I let go of trying to attain perfection.

The art of noticing is the first step; change comes after. It is huge that you have read this far, that you are willing to understand yourself, that part of you wants to live a little more kindly. I hope that you will recognize yourself in pieces of this book and that you'll learn you're not 'crazy' for feeling the way you do. I hope you'll start to understand that this was never your fault, that society drip-feeds us insecurities. I hope you'll start to see that there is a life outside of your worries. I hope you know that everything is changeable, that nothing is set in stone. I hope you know it's all going to be okay.

Having now learnt ways to placate the nastier side of my inner monologue, I find it ebbs and flows. Some days I appreciate the good in myself without a second thought, and some days the little voice convinces me that I'm worthless. But I'm okay with that; I'm only human. My end goal was never self-*love*; from the mindset I was in that seemed unachievable. Instead, I set my sights on a state of self-acceptance. No matter what, though, I've learned to stand tall. Not every day is a good day, but my inner monologue is no longer the dictator of that.

It will not happen overnight, but one day, when you're asked, 'what's one thing you like about yourself?', you won't want to curl up, to disappear. You'll be able to answer confidently. And even better, you'll believe the words you're speaking.

The process of becoming kinder to ourselves can feel overwhelming, and that's okay. For now, I want you to focus on simply listening, without judgement, to the beliefs you hold about yourself. Having huge realizations like, *oh, I've been bullying myself for years and I didn't even know!* can bring up heavy emotions, perhaps ones we've been avoiding. As we move into the beginning stages of tackling our inner critic and understanding our self-talk, I want you to know that it's okay if it feels like *a lot*. It's okay to put this book down, take a deep breath and come back to it tomorrow. In fact, that is an act of self-care in itself – to acknowledge when things feel too much and to be gentle with yourself. Also, please note, I'm not a medical professional or a doctor, so please seek care from professionals as and when you need it! There is no shame in asking for help. You are worthy of support.

The first step, noticing, can be agonizing. When I floated above my body that night and saw how I'd beaten myself down, I felt as though I was breaking. I felt grief for the years I'd lost and anger that I could ever have treated myself in that way. But the process of change begins with listening, noticing. To value your own needs is a huge first step.

Chapter 2
Unfriending Your Inner Critic

*Life is messy;
let it be messy.*

When you live your life by the rules of your inner critic, in fear of what might be said about you, of the flawed parts of yourself or of what could go wrong, you can become consumed by anxiety. You might spend all your time preparing for the things you are scared of happening that may never even happen, and that fear keeps you stuck. You may try to eliminate all threats and, in the process, shrink your life, until all that is left is you and your worries. At least, that is what happened to me.

Anxiety, biologically, exists to protect us from danger and to help us react to scary situations. When our amygdala – the part of our brain that's responsible for emotional reactions – flags up a perceived threat, it triggers our 'threat' response and effectively sends us into 'defence' mode, preparing us to successfully fight whatever danger is coming our way. This can be a very useful tool. It's quite reassuring to know that a part of our brain can detect threats that may endanger our lives. The issue, however, is that many of us have an over-excitable threat detector. And as culture and society has developed, our priorities and worries have too.

This combination of hyper-vigilance and ever-changing societal expectations is how the internal system that was built to help us fight off predators in the wild has begun to identify hypothetical, imagined social situations as a 'threat'.

There is nothing scarier for an insecure teenage girl than to be laughed at behind her back because she looked or acted a certain way. The overthinking spiral takes hold. The threat system's alarms blare in our minds and our bodies have to carry the stress of a human being chased by lions.

In my teenage years, I learned to tackle that anxiety with control. I wasted many hours trying to take charge of any variable in my life, of any flawed part of me that I could. My evenings were spent doing what, at the time, seemed like normal, harmless activities, the things I deemed hobbies that I now see were ways for me to squash the discomfort I felt in just being.

I turned to makeup tutorials on YouTube to be certain I wouldn't somehow 'do my makeup wrong' and be laughed at. I followed home workouts and manipulated my body into a size that would be immune to insults. I'd google everything I was unsure about in life so as to never step a foot out of line, to be sure that I followed the correct life protocol. I wanted to be unjudgeable.

Gradually, the strain I was putting on my body started to show. I was falling asleep in class, having panic attacks more days than not. I began to isolate myself because my self-esteem had dropped so low. The pursuit of perfection was exhausting.

My inner critic and I went through life hyper-aware of everything. We followed a set of rules, a regime, and it kept me safe.

The rules

Second-guess everything that's said to you, try to unpick if there's an insult buried in there.

Look at yourself through a critical lens – if I wanted to judge me, what would I focus on?

Notice everything. Notice the hairs out of place and the pores in your cheeks.

Then fix those things. Make sure they're hidden. Quick, before anybody else spots them too.

I was my own biggest critic so that I could pre-empt others' criticism. It was a foolproof technique, and it eased my anxiety. Until it didn't.

I struggled with friendships in every phase of school, and I never understood why I was always the one being pushed out. Ever the annoying one, the one who was 'too much'. The one who came into school on a Monday and found out that my friendship group hadn't invited me to the fun thing they had done over the weekend. I wish I'd known then what I know now – that just because the people around you don't understand every aspect of your layered, human self doesn't mean you are fundamentally flawed. It doesn't mean it's a *you* problem. It doesn't mean you need to change. It just means they aren't your people.

But I didn't know that then, and googling *'how to be less annoying'* doesn't provide quite as straightforward a toolkit as the millions of search results for altering your physical appearance. So, I turned to my inner critic to coach me. I decided that I'd dull myself down a little, show a little less of *me*. Be constantly conscious of how I was coming across, in every situation. I started to walk away from conversations replaying everything I'd said, highlighting every stutter or awkward pause, wondering what I could have said differently, cringing at the way things came out of my mouth.

I insulted myself in front of others – not for compliments, but so that everyone knew that I was *aware* I was ugly, because the idea of seeming as if I thought I was pretty, when I was actually ugly? Mortifying. I didn't even want to be perceived as confident. My self-esteem was so low and the fear of judgement ran so deep that I truly believed I had no right to confidence.

The worst thing about all of this is that none of it even slightly made a positive difference. The further I strayed from who I was, the worse I felt, the more anxious I became and the lower my confidence got. It's a phrase that's thrown around a lot but it's painfully true: you can't please everyone. You never will. You have to stop dedicating your life to trying to.

The only person whose judgement mattered was mine, but because I was so wrapped up in this voice of self-hatred, I was truly, deeply, miserable.

Taking every opportunity to focus on my imperfections wasn't conducive to a happy life, but my inner critic and I were so firmly intertwined that listening to its vitriol was no longer a choice. My fault-finding predisposition was no longer protecting me. I'd built myself a prison, and I was trapped.

Once you learn to recognize the voice of your negative self-talk, you can take the next step – unfriending your inner critic.

Criticizing yourself isn't serving you. There are, I'm sure, niche situations where it's a helpful strategy; times when a person genuinely needs to work on a destructive behaviour. But you are not, at your core, broken. You do not need fixing. You do not need to be hyper-aware of your faults to be a good person. Besides, is there such a thing as a 'good' person? Are we not all just humans, capable of doing good and bad things? Those thoughts aren't protecting you, helping you grow, or stopping you from messing up. They will keep you stuck. They will make you more and more insecure until you see no good in yourself. Life is messy; let it be messy.

That critical voice isn't your friend. You will be okay without it.

Finding your voice

What happened when I started to talk back to my inner critic shocked me. It was an awakening, a moment of clarity, a blindfold lifted from my eyes. I was in control of my own life. I was allowed to talk to myself in any which way I desired. There were few real rules in life, and yet I had lived so rigidly, obsessed with perfection.

One morning, seven months into my weight-gain journey, I found myself standing in my bedroom, just out of the shower. The harsh ceiling light was unforgiving on the reflection of my body, highlighting my cellulite and stretch marks – small signs of my body's healing. As I habitually did, I looked at myself in the mirror and heard the voice of my inner critic. It offered nothing new; its usual spiteful torments, which I'd tend to believe without question. My body hadn't changed since I'd lived this same moment the day before.

On this day, however, I shocked myself. I spoke up, spoke back. The inner critic told me that I looked horrific. I'd gained weight and I looked chubby and wrong and *ugly*. Most days,

I'd reach a point of overwhelm and would rush to hide my body in the baggiest clothes I could find, nauseous with self-hatred. But on this day, I found my voice. A quiet whisper, but that was something. I'd not so much as tried to fight the inner critic until now.

'It's just a body,' I told myself. 'Not good, not bad. I am looking after myself and eating what makes me happy, and my body will reflect that, and that is okay.'

Neutrality felt more palatable than positivity to me, which often cringed me out. Over time, I found myself standing up to my inner critic more and more often. Once I'd learned I was allowed to talk back, my whisper grew to a shout. It took time and practice, and I will explain just how I did it as we go through this book, but I became louder than my inner critic, and with that, I became so much happier.

Leaving the house got easier. Wearing less, or no, makeup started to feel okay. I began wearing clothes I liked even if I thought some people wouldn't. I stopped yelling at myself for small mistakes. I told myself things would be okay. I learned to recognize when I was in an overthinking spiral. I learned that, *no, my best friend of twenty years doesn't suddenly hate me* and, *no, I don't need to be awake until 2 a.m. worrying that she might*, and, *oh, my anxiety is lying to me*.

Social media, and the internet, has given reason to our inner critics in a way that can be confusing to untangle yourself from. Appearances have always been a commonplace worry, but we no longer feel pressure just to look good in day-to-day life, we are now also aware of the need to look Instagram-perfect for a photo that will freeze our flaws in time and live online, available to the world in a way that never existed before – to be zoomed in on, screenshotted, shared, liked, swiped past, scrutinized. Photographs are now less a way to capture memories and instead a method of documenting the times when we look our best – a means to show off flawless makeup, an outfit you hope you look good in, to declare that you have straight, white teeth, airbrushed skin, to be seen not for *who* you are, but *what* you are: a commodity.

Our inner critic is the brains behind the voice of our negative self-talk, drawing in information from the world around us to try to 'better' us, to save us from embarrassment. Subconsciously, when you're reading hateful comments about another woman's thighs, your inner critic is listening and learning, and you may start to worry about the way your thighs jiggle, or don't, depending on whatever body type is popular at that moment. When videos about 'make-up blindness' start trending, the inner critic knows it needs to worry a little more about how we do our makeup. When your mother looks in the mirror and uses the word fat to insult herself, the inner critic knows it cannot let you become fat.

I believe that insecurity is learned. For centuries, corporations have profited from breeding new insecurities and selling us products to fix them, capitalizing on more and more fictitious 'problems' and forming an ever-changing beauty standard. We spend our lives trying to conform to an ideal that, since the twentieth century, hasn't stayed consistent for longer than a decade. Both curvy and stick-thin figures have gone from worshipped, to despised, to sought after, then once again shunned in an alternating cycle on repeat.

Thanks to this incessant flitting between ideals, one thing that *has* stayed consistent is body image issues, which are particularly prevalent amongst women. Appearance anxieties are passed down through generations. Even if you'd never thought much of it before, hearing another person say they hate a feature of themselves that you also have teaches you to worry about it too. I didn't care about the size of my thighs until I learned that girls my age were desperate for thigh gaps. I didn't have one, and so the insecurity formed. For those of us who are sensitive and easily influenced, we can leave adolescence with an ingrained belief that there is always *something* we should be trying to change about ourselves.

But why? Why should you have to spend time trying to fix something that isn't broken? Why should you be insecure about something that *never* posed an issue in your life until somebody else said it should? Take this realization and use it to understand where your insecurities have stemmed from – this will change a lot for you. The insecurities of others is almost always what built the foundation of our own, whether they were insulting themselves, projecting onto you, or making unkind comments – it all ends up internalized.

In Another World

One question I like to ask myself when I feel my mind is spiralling with appearance anxiety, and one question I'd like you to ask yourself, is this:

> If nobody else existed on this Earth – would you worry about the things you worry about?

Of course, that one question, and the realization it hopefully triggers, cannot magic away your worries, but I do find it helpful to acknowledge that a lot of the stress and pressure we put ourselves under doesn't serve us at all. Your inner critic is forever going to be working against you, under the guise of working to better you.

Though it's difficult sometimes to pinpoint the exact origins of our anxieties, it can be a helpful exercise in helping us to let go of them. Ask yourself:

- What is one attribute that you find you're overly critical of yourself about? Can you recognize where that insecurity stems from, or where it first began?

- Were you insecure about this quality before somebody else deemed it a flaw – even if only in reference to themselves?

It can be easy to believe that being insecure is a personality fault, but I hope this exercise will help to demonstrate that your insecurities are not, and never were, your fault. This is not about pointing blame, but instead is a reminder to be gentle with yourself. Insecurities are learned, and they are a natural part of the human experience.

When you pick apart the origin of your insecurities, you'll probably realize they never started with you. Often, the things you criticize yourself for aren't because it's something you truly value, they're internalized opinions of the society you grew up in – the media, throwaway comments during childhood. Your inner critic may keep you stuck, afraid of letting go, of being your true self. It might insist you hate the face that came to be through generations of people loving one another. It tells you to hate the size of your arms, the arms that allow you to comfort the people you love. Hate the fact that you don't have a huge group of friends, despite being adored and cherished by those you're close to. Hate your smile and refuse to show it, despite it being so bright and so beautiful. Hate your body because it doesn't match the 'ideal body type', despite that being an ever-changing, impossible standard.

I hope in time that you can recognize just how pointless it is to pick yourself apart. Looking back at a younger version of myself, I realize that all that time spent trying to shrink myself could have been spent doing things that brought me joy. All that time I spent being miserable, exercising and restricting my food intake to achieve a figure I cannot healthily sustain, is time I cannot get back. And my hope is that fewer and fewer people will find themselves stuck in that same hellish trap.

I trained my inner critic to be on top form, to call me out for any small thing I needed to change, and I felt like it was protecting me. The feeling of permanently being one step ahead made me terrified to ignore any self-criticism. But just as I'd managed to train it to spot issues and help me fix them, I managed to train it out of that behaviour. I managed to build a new friend, this time a voice that offered me forgiveness, understanding and compassion in a way I'd never known before.

You deserve better than to be bullied by a voice inside your head. The insecurities you have formed throughout your life all have a root cause. As you begin to listen to yourself and start to unpick where those roots formed, you might just realize how baseless those insecurities are. It might just change your life! But more so, I hope you can start to find compassion for the version of you who first shaped these insecurities. It wasn't your fault that you grew up in a society riddled with insecurity. Both society and social media's profound obsession with appearance have made it borderline impossible to reach adulthood untouched by self-doubt.

Our black-and-white culture, in which everyone is innocent or guilty, good or bad, hot or not, leaves little room for us to exist in our grey areas. We are capable of doing wonderful things – and equally capable of doing harmful things – but we are not good or bad. We are humans, we are flawed. You do not owe it to anyone to be perfect, but you do owe it to yourself to be kind.

Is it an easy journey? No. But is it worth every single bit of hard work? A million times yes. Time spent hating ourselves is time wasted. Make time to heal, the time will pass anyway.

Chapter 3
The Comparison Trap

You can't hate yourself into being a person you love.

As a child, like many others I found the world big and scary and difficult to navigate. And as an adult, the world still feels big and scary and difficult to navigate, but with adulthood comes added pressure to manage it all with ease. I had assumed that adulthood would bring an innate understanding of how to handle life, which I've now learned doesn't really exist. In an ever-changing world, uncertainty is a constant. Comparing yourself to others can create an illusion that everyone else moves through life with ease, which is both isolating and untrue.

When you evaluate your own life, you might look around and see a world of high-achieving, perfectly presented people, all 'doing better than you' and seemingly gliding through the things you struggle with. You might enter a cycle of comparing your low moments to the highlights of others' lives, wondering why your struggles don't match up to what is actually a carefully constructed front. You may even think to yourself: *I wish I was like them*. And that is how the comparison trap is born.

The comparison trap is a trick of the mind. I call it *the comparison trap* because to me it is just that – a trap that is so easy to fall into and yet so difficult to escape. It lures us in with the highlights of others' lives, inviting us to criticize ourselves, our abilities and appearances, because we perceive everyone around us as more successful, beautiful or capable. As long as there are other humans on Earth, there will be means for you to make comparisons. The only escape from this is through self-acceptance.

It's common knowledge that children learn by example. But the observation of others' behaviour as a way to understand how to 'do life' isn't exclusive to childhood. As we grow older, we become able to think for ourselves, to make our own decisions and know what we like and dislike. As independent and capable as I may feel, we all, as humans, have an instinctive need to observe and evaluate other humans around us. It's how we learn and make sense of the world. Comparison is in our nature. Unknowingly, though, when we look to others' experiences for guidance in this way, we can find ourselves feeling as if we are falling behind.

Life is hard sometimes and it can be difficult to connect with your authentic self in a world that has such high expectations of us all. We are raised in a society where appearance comparison is encouraged. In Western culture, where tabloids consider famous women gaining weight, going makeup-free or merely ageing to be newsworthy, is it any wonder that we attach such importance to our appearance? Beauty pageants, trending body types, product after product invented, and marketed, to highlight flaws we have that we should change – we are raised to scrutinize every part of our appearance. And not just our appearance but our personality, too – we are told to not be too loud, but not too quiet; not too confident, but not insecure either; not too smart, but not unintelligent. The world around you demands that you be so many things at once. You're not self-obsessed, nor shallow, for responding to these pressures. You can't blame yourself for having an innate urge to compare yourself to others when society trains you to obsess over your every flaw.

Making comparisons about your appearance is a huge trap, and one I've fallen into many times. The appearance obsession is entwined in every part of popular culture. In things many of us mindlessly consume, like reality-TV dating shows, the inadvertent message is that love will find a person first at the hand of their appearance, then they can slowly show the less-important part of them – their personality. When aesthetics take such priority, you can lose sight of who you are. Ignoring a multitude of wonderful things within you, you can pick yourself apart and cast the focus on your body – the vessel that holds who you really are. Self-worth is now so tied up in our exterior that it's often difficult to see in ourselves the good that others can plainly see.

This toxic cocktail of societal expectations and subsequent shame has left many of us feeling unworthy of love and respect unless we meet conventional beauty standards and present a perfect personality alongside. But the restrictive framework of 'conventional beauty' is founded in the principles of white, heteronormative, able-bodied agencies, and so, by nature, it has led to a systematic exclusion and marginalization of countless individuals. It's unsurprising that so many people struggle with self-confidence in a society that prioritizes a specific, often genetically determined appearance. It's easy to look back now and understand that so much of my insecurity stemmed from that need to constantly compare myself to those around me. What wasn't so easy to understand then was that as imperfect and ever-changing humans, comparison is wasted energy. You will never be a direct replica of the girl you wish you looked like. You will always be you – which is a wonderful thing!

But I promise you this: your body is the least-interesting thing about you. And, more importantly, you can't hate yourself into being a person you love.

As a child, I loved the idea that we were all unique and different, wonderfully human. I took such joy in observing the personal choices we all made, that everyone had their own favourite colour, or subject, or hobby. I was fascinated by the notion that we were all our own individual people, going home to different lives. And yet, the older I got, the more I noticed that we were all trying to become carbon copies of each other. Everyone wanted the same exact body type – skinny but not *too* skinny, a small waist but with boobs and a bum. There was a correct way to style your hair, a correct length of skirt, a bag that was cool, a bag that wasn't cool. I had a head of curly hair which refused to be styled and, because it was different, I hated it.

The terror that I felt about looking different, or being out of place, held control over me. I wasn't alone in that feeling but I didn't know that then and it was an incredibly isolating experience. It seemed as though everyone was breezing through school with some unspoken knowledge of how to just 'be' and I never got the memo.

I wanted, more than anything, to look like everyone else around me, to wear the things that were cool, to have clear skin, to be perfect, and pretty, and not too clever but clever enough, and likeable, and popular, and everything that I thought made up the ideal person. Reflecting on my time at school, I realize that even as a young teen, the weight that a person's appearance held was huge. Most people didn't care if you were 'nice', or a good friend. They didn't care if you were clever and caring. They cared if you were pretty. They cared if your shoes were cool and if your makeup was flawless, and whether you'd be embarrassing to be seen to be friends with.

Surviving school and avoiding bullying meant fitting in. And fitting in meant observing what everyone else was doing and wearing and recreating it in order to be accepted. Comparing myself to others was an essential part of survival, feeding into that inner critic, my hateful inner monologue. An anxious teenager with an inferiority complex, I wanted to be liked so desperately, yet I didn't like myself.

By the end of my time at school, my life had ventured down such a different path to everyone else in my year group. I had ended up in hospital, unable to sit my exams, stuck within the walls of a psychiatric unit while my peers enjoyed their extended summer break. I had no choice but to radically accept that I was, and would always be, different. I see now how none of my worries about being cool meant anything at all, how it was all just a game of keeping up appearances, how superficial the popularity hierarchy was. But at the time you can't see that. No matter how many times an older person tells you 'school is such a small part of your life in the grand scheme of things', or, 'you'll not even remember that these awful things happened in a few years' time' – it doesn't mean anything, because you are there, in the middle of it, feeling it all. You often cannot see past the wall of com--parison, the judgement, the fear of being shown up.

At the time I didn't know that what I was doing was actively comparing myself to everyone, I thought I was discovering myself. I was at an age where my brain was still developing, meaning I was extremely impressionable and vulnerable to messaging. Society's unrealistic expectations, coupled with constant comparison to those at the same stage of life as me, only cemented my negative beliefs about myself and the world. I thought it was me learning how to be a teenager. Really, I was learning how to squish myself into spaces I wasn't meant to fit.

Comparison, still, ate into every part of my life, even after I'd left school. I had an obsession with losing weight that was coupled with raging body dysmorphia, and I managed to convince myself that every person I saw, ever, was skinnier than me. I didn't follow the traditional life path that I saw so many others venture down and flourish on – school, college, uni, a conventional job – and so I compared myself, feeling worthless, useless; as if I was going nowhere in life because everyone else was just doing *so much better than I was*. And then there's social media, which, despite the good it can bring, is a place where you can use literal numbers to directly compare yourself to your peers.

Your Green-Eyed Friend

Comparison is in our nature, and it can often lead to feeling jealous. Jealousy, although it is often perceived as negative, is a normal response in life.

So let's confront this feeling. Get comfortable wherever you're sitting and close your eyes. Without putting any judgement upon yourself, ask yourself this: do you notice comparison showing up in your life?

For example, when you feel proud of something you've done, how often do you jump to thinking of others who you feel have done better/more than you? Or, if you could wave a magic wand and instantly be granted a quality or attribute that somebody else has, what would it be? What story do you tell yourself which leads you to believe their version is 'better' or more desirable than yours? Do you find yourself feeling jealous of those you perceive to be better than you, and if so, do you feel shame around acknowledging your jealousy?

Jealousy is often perceived to be a negative thing, but until an emotion is used to hurt or harm another person or oneself, it is just an emotion. It is neutral. We don't need to beat ourselves up for feeling human emotions.

If you could speak to the part of you that engages in comparison, what would you say to it? What does it need to hear? What kindness can you offer that part of you?

> Confronting comparison can feel uncomfortable because often we have to look directly into the parts of us that feel inferior, or inadequate. It's completely okay if this feels difficult; you are not a bad person for experiencing jealousy, or for comparing yourself to others. Comparison is hugely tied up in self-worth, and with that, self-talk. Through learning how to talk to yourself with compassion, and to believe in the good within you, I hope you will start to see how wonderfully you are doing, and how limiting negative comparison is.

The comparison trap is a hellish place to be, but we can use it to our advantage. Over the past few years of my life, I've learned to take my comparative thoughts and recognize that another person's beauty is not an absence of my own. I decided to reframe them, to start adding a variant of 'and so am I' onto the end of my comparative thoughts. *She's so beautiful – and so am I! She's got a really cool style – and so do I, we're just different!* I've grown to celebrate the fact that I'm *not* the people I compare myself to. I don't need to put myself, or anyone else, down in order to feel good about myself. I can turn my comparison into compliments and that positive energy spreads out into my own thoughts about myself. It's easy to imagine that everyone is saying horrible things about you if you are thinking so negatively and competitively. But when you start to change them into positive, complimentary thoughts that are neutral about yourself, it opens you up to the reality – that *what if people think I'm ugly?* can also sound like *what if people think I'm beautiful?*

Jealousy can also highlight the things that we feel are lacking in our lives, and in turn allow us to make positive change. For example, a thought like, *I'm jealous she has so many friends,* may signify a feeling of loneliness in your own life. And that's okay: jealousy, like all emotions, is neutral. Uncomfortable emotions are simply invitations to listen to ourselves and understand why we might be struggling.

I'm now in an era of my life where I think people who are uniquely, unapologetically themselves are the coolest people you'll meet. That doesn't mean you have to be groundbreakingly eccentric, but the ability to be true to yourself is wonderful. I think I am cool, and I like my style, and I like my curly hair. The fact that I don't directly resemble a single one of my friends is a breath of fresh air. Letting go of the pressure to fit the mould of every single person my age was like breaking out of chains I didn't realize were restricting my growth. For so many years, I thought I'd lost the chance to ever really know myself, or to be able to feel comfortable in who I was. The idea of being myself both exhilarated and terrified me, but the journey to becoming my true self has been such a beautiful unveiling, one that has changed my view of the world and allowed me to feel at home in my body.

I've never been more me. How absurd is it that being *me* used to be the one thing I wished I wasn't?

My favourite compliment to receive is that I'm interesting. I'm layered. How could I ever want to dull myself down when the best relationships in my life exist because I show up with all my selves, with all my quirks, and when my favourite friendships are those with zero pressure? I never have to be somebody I'm not. I have full permission to be me. And I love the version of me that those people bring out.

One afternoon, as we strolled through the park, a friend and I were chatting about how hard it was to not compare ourselves to people our age. I opened up about how I couldn't escape the feeling that I was so behind our peers, and though, in my eyes, she was one of the peers I felt behind, she said she felt the same. And then came five words that altered the way I viewed comparison altogether. It was one of the first things that had ever broken the walls of my comparison cycle. They were words said so casually, but the impact they had on me was huge:

'I compare myself to you.'

For the version of me I was then – so insecure, with such a low view of myself – I couldn't comprehend anybody comparing themselves to me. It shifted something in my brain. In that moment, I realized: you compare yourself to people who also compare themselves to you.

It seemed totally absurd, having always viewed myself as the ugliest, the worst, the bottom of the barrel in any category I put myself in. I couldn't imagine anyone liking anything about me, let alone comparing themselves to me. But here's the thing: we are all capable of falling victim to the comparison trap. We all have insecurities. Every single person you walk past on the street would be able to tell you something they didn't like about themselves. And somebody else will always have the version of that thing they wish they had. For somebody, at some point, you will have been that person. Living with low self-esteem makes it seem laughable that others could be comparing themselves to us in the same way that we are to them. Laugh all we like, it's happening. The phrase 'we always want what we don't have' rings true for every person I know in my life.

I realized I wasn't comparing myself to those around me because I actually embodied all the horrible things I believed I did, I was comparing myself because I was human. Everyone was comparing themselves to everyone else. We were all insecure in some way, because we had been taught to be. We were taught that it was brash to acknowledge things we liked about ourselves. We were taught that we were a constant improvement project. We were taught to not just be okay in ourselves, that there was always *something* we could fix.

There have likely been times throughout your life where a friend has said they don't like what they're wearing, how their hair looks that day, maybe that their skin looks bad, anything superficial and appearance-related. And there have likely been times where, while they've felt that way, you've either liked the thing they're insecure of, or haven't noticed it at all. Humans see things differently. Your eyes aren't 'right' and others' wrong; beauty is subjective. *Feeling* ugly doesn't mean you're ugly. Our insecurities feel so huge in our own minds, and yet, the likelihood is that nobody else is thinking the things you're thinking about yourself.

For so long, I'd used my obsessive comparison to talk down to myself on the daily, used it as proof, evidence, that I was less than others, that I wasn't as worthy of good things, that I'd never be loved. Suddenly I saw it for what it was, a nasty voice in my head. Comparison fed the hateful nature of my inner monologue, but it didn't need to.

Bring to mind a person in your life who you love spending time with. Ask yourself – what is it about them that brings you joy? Is it the size of their waist, their toned stomach, their perfect hair that first comes to mind? Or is it the way they make you laugh, or how they always listen and care, or the memories you have together? If you are like me, it'll be the latter. I know not one person in my life whose appearance I value over their personality. Put bluntly, the connection we make between looking good and being loveable is unfounded. A mirror cannot reflect back at you the reasons why you are loved.

No friend worth having is choosing to spend their time with you because you have a thigh gap. You aren't more fun to be around because you have clear skin. Nobody will remember you for the car you drove or the exam results you received. It's only our internal narrative that inflates the significance of our appearance, and our appearance only matters as much as we let it. The comparison trap doesn't have an end, it is a cycle that you will be stuck in forever unless you decide to accept yourself. You deserve more than a life spent comparing yourself to others, wishing you were somebody else, when the person you are is already wonderful and worthy of happiness.

Chapter 4
Insecurity Is Lonely

You can be loved even when you feel unloveable.

Within the pink-painted walls of my teenage best friend's bedroom, I'd grown to feel comfortable, safe to be a little more me. I lay in a tangle of blankets, groggy from avoiding sleep together the night before, still coming down from a pick-'n'-mix-induced sugar high. Though I couldn't switch off my self-consciousness altogether, my body felt safe to relax here. I normally knew better than to show the hyper side of myself, the reason I'd been labelled annoying as a child, but in the presence of my best friend, I let myself go a little.

We had the sort of friendship where twelve hours together felt like twenty minutes. I felt my social battery recharge in the hours we spent laughing and talking about everything and nothing. My inner critic, however, convinced me that she too would get sick of me. It regularly reminded me that everyone did, eventually.

In the soft sunlight, caught off guard by the safety of our friendship, I let myself laugh too loud, a bundle of suppressed energy escaping me and unveiling my hyper side, the part of me I tried to keep hidden. I'd let myself exist with no limits for a brief moment, and I was jolted from my insouciant state. My inner critic was there, loud, in my ear.

My body was alert again. I became conscious of myself as a wave of self-loathing washed over me. For a second, I'd stopped controlling every aspect of myself, and I was too much, I'd let myself get too confident. I shrank back into myself.

Cheeks flushed pink, mind flooding with the thoughts I knew everyone else had about me, I uttered the words I said so often: 'I'm so annoying, sorry.'

Usually it went unnoticed and the conversation moved on. I felt peace in knowing I'd acknowledged I was aware I was annoying. As if it absolved me of being talked about behind my back, because I was in on the opinion too. But this time, my friend rolled her eyes.

'Ro, it's so much more annoying when you say you're annoying.'

Those words punched me in the stomach and then turned me inside out. *Oh, God.* First of all, I'd had what was simultaneously my worst fear and the very thing I so believed to be true, confirmed – I *was* annoying those around me. Second of all, I'd been apologizing for being annoying for so long. Nobody had ever told me that that was also annoying. *How many people had I embarrassed myself in front of by saying that? How many people thought I was weird and annoying, even more so because I said I was annoying? How do you apologize for being annoying when that's annoying in itself? How do you stop being annoying? How do you apologize for apologizing too much if you can't apologize anymore? And then how do I apologize for apologizing for apologizing so much?*

This is the thing about self-deprecation. Much like comparison, it doesn't serve us in the way we think it does. We are, more often than not, entirely fabricating opinions of ourselves and then deciding, with unwavering certainty, that other people are thinking them. As an anxious, hyper-sensitive person, I have always lived as though I possess an incredible, rare talent in the art of knowing what others are thinking. And in my life, this has only built barriers within my relationships.

I used to gather every glimmer of evidence, any hint that supported my 'everyone hates me' theory – a joke not laughed at, a slightly unusual eye movement – and lay them under the microscope of my critic to determine how others perceived me. Whether it was true or not, I usually found ways to make things fit my narrative. I formed a confirmation bias, a habit of searching for, and only believing, the facts that confirmed what I already thought. I processed everything in a way that aligned with my mindset. I convinced myself I was right.

I wish I could talk to that version of me and ask, isn't it a little suspicious that the opinions you assume others hold are *always* negative? It's a little strange that you somehow reach the conclusion that you're annoying *every time*, that you must be hated, is it not? Could it be … no, surely not … that your anxious predisposition has hijacked your trusty vibe reader? Or that you are projecting? Perhaps your negative self-talk is interjecting here? I couldn't see it then, but I was allowing my own negative feelings about myself to influence my perception of those around me.

That's what insecurity can do. It decides that the way we feel about ourselves *must* be the way everyone else feels, too. It can be the reason we withdraw from friendships entirely, the reason we can't be ourselves around anyone else, the reason we never let our guard down enough to find true friendship. Insecurity is lonely and it's exhausting.

Before we have the chance to realize it, our negative self-talk can weave its way into our relationships, causing rifts and creating divides. I do not agree with the phrase 'you have to love yourself before you can love somebody else', because I loved before I was healed, and I know that love was whole, but I do believe it makes it a hell of a lot harder to be loved when you are constantly denying that you are deserving of it.

My inner critic was very talented in convincing me I was not deserving of love. When I couldn't see the good in myself, my inner critic convinced me that I was a fraud, and, at my core, a terrible person. I lived in fear of everyone who loved me suddenly realizing that too, despite having no real evidence to support my worry. This fear drove a wedge between me and the love that others gave me. It was only when I learned to listen to myself that I understood the roots to the anxiety I held about the people in my life suddenly seeing my 'true colours'. My self-esteem was so low, my self-talk so negative, that I couldn't believe the good others saw in me. My deep-seated belief that I was lazy, unkind and awkward, to me meant that they were all being fooled by my mask.

Through noticing that this tangle of anxieties and fears was why I'd put my guard up for so long, I could allow myself to first work on the base of those worries, and then on opening my heart to those around me and accepting the love and help they offered.

Relationships can help us to heal and grow, just as mine have. You can be loved even when you feel unloveable. Unknowingly, however, you may put up barriers. You may hide parts of yourself that others would love to see, or you will push people away when they're nice to you. And, as I learned the hard way, you might annoy people by vocalizing your self-hatred.

As I've grown and learned to view myself through a different lens, a far less self-critical one, I have also awoken to the fact that it's quite unfair to put thoughts in others' heads. Half the people I've assumed would be thinking horrible things about me have been tarred with the same brush as girls who genuinely were mean to me, and yet these people were lovely, the sort who'd never talk badly about somebody behind their back. It wasn't fair on them, really, to assume their heads would be filled with such vitriol about me. I don't blame myself because I know that it was my inner critic, the voice of my negative self-talk, who had total control over me back then. I can't take back my excessive apologies, my 'are you mad at me?' spiels, or the hours spent panicking that being left on read meant my entire circle of friends no longer wanted me around.

It wasn't my fault, nor a flaw of my personality, I was living with a bully in my brain and it warped the way I saw things, and people, around me.

My teenage years unfolded in a way that meant I lost friends, and for a long time I felt quite isolated. As I've found new people, my people, and have learned to talk to myself in a nicer way, I can see that the behaviours I apologized for back then weren't anything more than me just being myself and are certainly not behaviours I'd find annoying now. Back then, I was living on a livewire, attuned to any small thing I did that could later come back to shock me.

I now know I am deserving of love. I know I am flawed, which is part and parcel of being human, but regardless, I have a lot of good in me. I do not need to work to be loved.

I do not need to perform to be liked. I do not need to exert all my energy existing behind a mask, drained of what makes me *me*, dulling myself down to be likeable. I am likeable to the right people. I am loved by those who love me. And all of these things are true for you, too. You deserve to believe it, and I hope one day you will. When I tune into my body now, when I listen to my self-talk, it is no longer riddled with social anxieties. I notice the good in relationships I have, I notice the small ways in which people show me they care for me. I have made peace with the fact I will not be everyone's person – everyone is not my person. Not every human is compatible, and it took me a long time to understand that. The notion that it was unrealistic to want everyone in life to like me was a hard pill to swallow.

One of the beautiful things that will happen when you become secure in yourself is becoming comfortable with being unable to control others' perceptions of you. If they don't find you interesting, or funny, or likeable, let them not like you. You will find the people who want to hear what you have to say. You will be liked by people, and if you feel you are not, know you simply haven't found your people yet.

As I grew more able to engage in positive self-talk, I found myself less trapped inside my head and more present in the moment. Throughout this journey, I hope you will feel that too. Life is too precious to have time with loved ones overshadowed by a nagging worry that they secretly don't like you. We will talk more about noticing negative patterns within relationships and setting boundaries in Part Two of this book (page 73), but as you learn to listen to yourself, you may realize some of the relationships in your life are leaving you feeling drained, or more critical of yourself. Part of listening to yourself is realizing that forcing yourself to be someone you're not is an energy-drainer. As we move into changing our self-talk, you may notice friendships where you are not wholly yourself, or where you are more unkind to yourself, and it is okay to feel you need to limit those. Society doesn't teach us to put ourselves first, but self-care isn't selfish.

I know I am my favourite version of myself when I am happy and relaxed, when the mask is off, when I am loud and perceived and okay with being under a spotlight. My relationships thrive when I am true to who I am, and when those I am with welcome every side to me.

I had to be kind to myself in order to feel kindness from others. I had to stop projecting my narratives onto others in my life in order to feel safe in friendships. I had to tell myself, night after night, that my friends were sleeping soundly and not replaying something I said that came out slightly awkwardly, that everyone else moves on because it's only me who cares this much, that I wasn't hated and that if people didn't want to be around me, they wouldn't.

Living in the moment and refusing to ruminate on my interactions earlier in the day is what I make a priority now. Living in the past serves nobody.

Rewind and Reflect

Many people engage in similar thinking patterns to those that I used to, so I'd like to share a realization I had which I largely credit for the fact that I no longer overthink every friendship I have.

I'd like you to think about a person in your life who you've felt that you've annoyed before. Perhaps it's just a fleeting thought, or perhaps you've found yourself replaying your time together, scrutinizing yourself for what you said, how you acted, and so on. Have you only met up with them once?

If so, fine, perhaps they just weren't your person.

If not, think about this: we are humans with free will. We are capable of saying no to seeing people. We don't have to spend our free time with people we don't enjoy being with. People are under no obligation to stay your friend. They can leave if they want to. If they were all really thinking the way we fear they are, wouldn't they have left by now? Is this not, perhaps, just our negative self-beliefs taking the steering wheel?

You are not responsible for everyone's happiness. You cannot control how others' brains work, or how you are perceived, you can only control how you behave. Stop wasting your energy and sabotaging your relationships because your brain is misfiring. I promise, letting your guard down can be a beautiful thing.

Throughout this section of the book, I hope you have started to notice the way that you talk to yourself and the thought patterns that may be holding you back from showing yourself the kindness you deserve. Though it isn't going to be an overnight fix, the fact that you have picked up this book and have the willingness to be gentler with yourself, is a wonderful achievement.

You may not realize it, but the ember of hope that I spotted within me all those years ago, the little fire that sparked such positive change in my life, is also within you. There may be parts of you that have been hurt throughout your life, forming worries and insecurities. Sometimes those hurt parts can get a little stuck and need some nurturing, but the first step is to acknowledge their existence, to listen to the story they tell through our self-talk. In Part 2, we are going to begin to guide our self-talk into a more positive space, to find a life where our minds are peaceful places, where the voices in our brains can be our friends, not bullies.

A life spent hating yourself is no life at all.

Part 2
Talk to Yourself

Perhaps Part 1 has opened your eyes to an inner world of negative self-talk, or perhaps it affirmed what you already knew about yourself. Whichever is true, I hope you found some comfort in seeing you're not alone, that others' brains work like yours do, but mostly that self-confidence is possible, even for people who have only known self-hatred. As we begin Part 2 and dive into the more practical chapters, I want to remind you that you can take this book at a pace that works for you. If you feel overwhelmed at any point, put it down, breathe, and take a moment away. This book is here to help you.

We are now going to delve into the intentional action I took against my negative self-talk, the ways I learned to be kind to myself in the midst of self-hatred, and how healing and happiness is possible for you, too.

Chapter 5
Unlearning Shame

You don't owe the world an apology.

The more open and vulnerable I've allowed myself to be with those around me, the more I have come to realize how common so many of the 'embarrassing' experiences I have are. Almost every conversation I've had in which I've confessed to something 'shameful' about myself, that I do or have done, has ended with another person lighting up and saying, 'oh my goodness, me too'. Being vulnerable and sharing the parts of myself I am not proud of, has enabled myself and others to connect, and to take a long exhale as I realize that I no longer need to feel shame – I am not alone and you aren't either.

Shame, I've found, is the curse of being a sensitive soul. It is an isolating place to be, stuck within an emotion tied to things we feel we cannot speak about. It is red hot and burning, it is the nausea in your stomach and the shiver down your spine. It doesn't discriminate but knows how to wreak havoc in the minds of overthinkers. Shame can keep you up at night, can hand you blame for things for which you owe no apology. And, more often than not, if you are an overthinker, you can do the mental gymnastics it takes to justify the shame you feel.

Guilt and shame are often confused. While guilt is an emotion directly linked to an action and can help us rightfully recognize our mistakes (*I did something bad*), shame is a persistent, punitive feeling, the voice that convinces you: *I am, at my core, bad*. Shame can manifest less as a response to a specific action, and more as a gradually ingrained belief. I find much of my shame is rooted in the word 'should' – *I should have done more today, I should be skinnier, I should have clearer skin, I shouldn't struggle in this way*. It is the by-product of the constant focus on our shortcomings, rather than our strengths.

Shame shows up in thoughts that surface, like, *I am ashamed to be myself*, even if you can't really place why you feel that way. For people who already hold negative self-beliefs, it can serve as confirmation. In situations that may evoke a warranted, short-term feeling of guilt that can be processed and moved past for some, those with low self-esteem may internalize their guilt, compounding their shame and endorsing their negative beliefs, further shrinking the sense of self.

Shame, much like our inner critic, can be both intrusive and go undetected. Though many people do not realize that what they are feeling is shame, it can sit in the background, feeding into our anxieties, and this perpetual feeling of shame plays a significant role in shaping an intoxicating mindset that many of us feel trapped in.

Low self-worth and shame reinforce each other. As your self-worth becomes tangled up in shame's lies, your opinion of yourself sinks lower, and shame feeds on your negative self-belief. It's a feeling that clings to you, one that becomes entwined with your self-image, and if you do not break free of shame, it will grow with you. Shame often prompts us into a negative self-talk spiral, it can make us withdraw from those around us and lead us to fundamentally believe *I am bad* despite the absence of any wrongdoing. I am an advocate for feeling our feelings, but if you don't challenge your shame you will become stuck in a constant reinforcement of your negative opinions, and that will only serve to harm you.

As I walked through the doors of the building where I went to be weighed each week, a flood of panic threatened to engulf me. This was not a new feeling, but it never got easier.

'You can face away; you don't have to see the number.' My nurse reminded me with a kind smile, just as she did at every weigh-in appointment.

I nodded and pulled off my shoes, never untying the laces because I knew I'd want to slip them back on and leave as quickly as possible when this was over. It was a wasted reminder, though I knew I'd be happier if I listened, I couldn't bear the idea of somebody else knowing my weight when I didn't. Both knowing and not knowing were torture, but my need for 'control' came out on top.

With great reluctance, I placed one foot after another on the base of the scales. My stomach churned as I stood, unintentionally holding my breath, waiting for the number to appear.

'Okay.' My nurse said, turning to write a number I wished she didn't know in her book. A bead of sweat rolled down my back. I stared blankly at my weight, feeling my cheeks grow pink as I stepped off the scales.

'How do you feel about that?' she asked.

Pushing my feet back into my shoes, I shrugged. I didn't want to talk about it.

The honest answer was: shame. I felt shame for the fact I'd gained weight. I felt shame for having an illness that would make that number the focus of my next week. I felt shame for the fact I felt shame. I felt shame for the fact I was here at all.

When I, as a young girl entrenched in an eating disorder, stood on the scales and the number that flashed up told me I'd gained weight, I felt ashamed. I hadn't done anything *wrong*, though. I was applying a harsh judgement to a morally neutral event because society had taught me that weight gain was something to fear. That feeling of shame was a fire inside me, and as it burned, I found myself throwing all positive beliefs I held about myself into the flames. Shame demanded my attention, told me to hate myself, to repent, to compensate for the fact my body had changed. My guilt was drastically unjustified, but shame wouldn't let me see that. I had learned from society that the most important thing about me was my body, and although that is untrue, my body changing shattered my self-image. As an impressionable teen, I took these wrongly informed, shame-riddled thoughts as facts, as I often did with my feelings. I left that room and spent the next week punishing myself in desperation to rid myself of this nauseating feeling of shame.

A shame-filled world

50 best and worst beach bodies!

Stars lose fight with cellulite!

'Ruining their looks': celebrities' pictures before and after weight gain.

These were the headlines of magazines you'd find in hair salons, the supermarket and on coffee tables in the 2000s. The public humiliation of famous women for ageing and gaining weight was par for the course. I have no doubt that those sorts of headlines were a huge contributor to the widely held view that body changes are 'bad' and that we should view them as some sort of treachery, deserving of guilt, a reason to carry shame.

For anyone who grew up in the 70s, 80s, 90s and 2000s, there was no avoiding the media's blatant fatphobia and body shaming. It's no surprise so many people have internalized these beliefs.

The majority of us were spoon-fed negative associations with weight gain from our earliest experiences of socialization, subliminally taught that our appearance should be of great concern. As a result, many of us have at some point fallen victim to this agenda, willingly or not. Society's priorities have led us astray, and as a result, guilt, embarrassment and shame have left a multitude of people crippled by low self-esteem.

Embarrassment is one of the founding emotions in the development of shame. In my experience, embarrassment feels warmer than guilt, but equally as unpleasant – less associated with an action being morally wrong, and more as a result of something unintentional that goes against societal norms and expectations. The two are not mutually exclusive, but where guilt feels heavy and cold, embarrassment feels softer. And yet, experiencing either can lead to internalized shame.

This is not to label feelings good or bad, because I am very much an advocate for embracing all of our feelings without judgement. All emotions serve a purpose. There are times when guilt is a reasonable emotional response, for example, if you do something that hurts others. A manageable level of guilt can help you learn and grow. Shame, however, keeps us stuck in a self-hateful space. Would you tell teenage me, who gained some weight and consequently stopped fitting into her jeans, that she should feel shame? Would you tell a person suffering with acne (an uncontrollable skin condition) to be embarrassed about their skin? Should having stretch marks, which simply showcase how our bodies have grown, be a reason to feel guilt? The answer is no – and yet so many people wouldn't see how damaging it is to hold these beliefs about themselves. Too many people are punishing themselves for being human, burdened by the crushing weight of these feelings. I struggle to see how our natural ageing process, or the cellulite on our thighs, or the fact that we are not born airbrushed, are things deserving of such a punitive feeling.

Somewhere along the way, as the pressure to be perfect took its seat at the front of many of our minds, feelings of shame around parts of us we deemed not good enough have gone unquestioned. The importance you may have attached to physical attributes, which in the grand scheme of things are totally irrespective of a person's character, make this shame seem valid. But it's not just physical appearance we critique unfairly, and I for one have been guilty of labelling the person I am unkindly. Too loud, too awkward, too clever, too quiet, too confident, too much and yet simultaneously forever feeling not enough. You are enough. And the only thing you're 'too much' of is hard on yourself. There is no way to please everybody; instead, try to be somebody *you* like. The person you are right now is somebody to be proud of.

Each time I see a new appearance-critiquing trend appear online, or can hear shame in the way somebody speaks about their body, I feel the urge to scream 'WHO CARES?' Why are we living miserably, in constant inner turmoil, over things that are so superficial?

Who is served by this shame and insecurity? Who benefits from us hating ourselves, really? I ask myself this every time I notice myself putting judgement on my appearance or my personality. Living in the shackles of your personal shame will only hold you back and distract you from your true potential. There is so much life outside of shame. There is so much to experience, to feel, to learn; so many people to meet and places to go. Letting shame dictate your days isn't how life is meant to be lived. And you may not realize this is what you are doing, but if you have thoughts like, 'I'll visit the beach once I'm happy in my body', that is shame talking. That being said, I understand just how tricky it is to break free when negative self-talk is all you've ever known. The first step, as mentioned in Chapter 1, is noticing. All beliefs we hold about ourselves stem from somewhere. Until we begin to unpick the capitalist origins of society's heavy judgement on appearance, we will continue to deem certain human aspects as 'bad' without question.

As we briefly touched on in Chapter 2, society has a long history of exhibiting and exploiting human flaws, particularly those of women, to invent superfluous problems and sell solutions. This regime, creating a cycle of self-doubt and consumerism, plants new seeds of shame in hopes to turn a profit for the companies who can sell 'miracle' cures ... for things that were never an issue before the media decided they were.

A prime example of this is the 'hip dip' trend, which I would have fallen victim to during the years I was battling with my body image. Hip dips, if you, like I was, are confused, are the slight indentations in our hips, above our thighs. They are a completely normal part of the human body's bone structure. Out of nowhere, I began to see articles and videos more and more frequently, some of young girls expressing how they hate their hip dips, others detailing how to get rid of your hip dips altogether. The most ludicrous part about it? Whether or not you have prominent hip dips is determined by your genetics, your bone structure and your body's natural distribution of fat. There is no exercise you can do, no diet you can follow, that will successfully rid you of your anatomical bone structure. And though science says that it is entirely natural and healthy to have hip dips, there are products you can pay for to remove them. I saw fitness courses sold with a promise of 'no more hip dips'. I saw injectable cosmetic treatments suggested to achieve 'smoother, sexier hips'. When you search 'products that get rid of hip dips fast', one of the first results is a skin-tightening cream. Though I am no doctor, I can say with certainty that there is no way a *cream* in a pretty pink tub is capable of altering your body's bone structure.

I am so glad that when this trend arose I had the awareness and ability to know that this was a trend invented to sell more products, and that my hip dips were perfectly fine and here to stay. Without my total body neutrality, I could have easily absorbed the shame that comes with seeing a part of your body spoken about in a derogatory way online.

I could list five hundred more examples of capitalism's subtle influences and sales tactics, but case studies are not the point – the point is that you did not learn to feel shame about your appearance because there is a genuine problem with it. You learned to feel shame about your appearance because every time you buy a product to try to ease that feeling of shame, you are lining the pockets of a CEO heading up one of the many corporations in the beauty industry.

Shame around our appearance is one issue, but then comes the shame cast upon women who dare to *not* feel shame. People who dare to be happy in their skin.

'She's cocky.'
'She's so sure of herself.'
'She's obsessed with herself.'

The discourse around people who are brave enough to admit to liking themselves is quite unforgiving, at least it has been in my experience. It's further evidence that you can't win if you're living to please others: if society successfully shames you into changing your appearance, when you finally feel good about yourself, you'll be shamed for that too. But strangers' opinions don't mean that self-confidence isn't worthwhile, it absolutely is. The key is to look inward, rather than outward. The term self-confidence is 'self' confidence for a reason – you cannot rely on the approval of others to feel good in yourself; acceptance of yourself will only come from within.

Many of us have found ourselves trapped in a shame cycle: even if you bought into the marketing, you are not allowed to reap the rewards. Should you try to change yourself as a result of shame and finally achieve the mythical appearance-joy they sell you, you may be ridiculed for daring to like yourself. It is one of society's strangest paradoxes that the media sells a dream of finding confidence in ourselves even though you may be ridiculed for expressing it.

When you've grown accustomed to the way confident people are perceived, grappling with the idea of starting to let go and to accept yourself can feel worrisome. Judgement has long been thrust on people who dare to speak highly of themselves. And not just on people who have high self-esteem, but anyone who makes a statement in the way they dress, who lives in a bigger body and refuses to feel embarrassed about that, who doesn't align with the values and standards society has set.

It's scary to face up to a system as old as time. It takes guts to say no, that actually, they're wrong – it isn't cocky, or embarrassing, or self-obsessed to not spend a lifetime at war with ourselves.

The more we embrace ourselves, and the more we call out others on their outdated opinions, the less shameful it will feel. Self-love isn't conceited. I do not judge the women I see taking selfies in the street. I do not judge the girls who say, 'I look good today'. I do not judge the people who can pull off outfits I'd be nervous to wear. I do not judge them, but I also don't judge those who do, because judgement stems from a place of unhappiness. You do not need to feel shame if you find yourself judging others, but it may be helpful to understand why you lean towards doing so. The discourse around self-confidence needs to become much more encouraging. If it isn't hurting anyone, why is there such spite around it? Why do we feel such an aversion to it? Why is confidence so overly conflated with egotism?

Unlearning the human instinct to judge others helps us let go of our own shame. In letting go of shame, we make room for so much positivity – with less overthinking, less panic about perfection, fewer negative spirals about the size of our thighs or hips or stomach, more time can be spent with those we love, making memories, or helping our communities, or building a new hobby, or being fully present in a relationship and watching it flourish.

To reach a place where shame no longer has a hold over us, we first need to notice when we are experiencing feelings of shame.

Looking Shame in the Eye

Close your eyes and think back to the last time you remember feeling shame. If you can't bring to mind any one event, is there anything that has made you feel uncomfortable within yourself recently? Has anything brought up that skin-crawling, uncomfortable, want-to-hide-away feeling for you? If so, did this feeling reinforce a deeper belief you hold about yourself?

What was that experience? What factors contributed to you feeling shame, was it perhaps because others were around at the time?

To help visualize this, you could draw a basic flow chart with a few words describing the experience at the top, then the feelings that accompanied it, then any other situations you've been in that this reminded you of, and any beliefs that you hold about yourself that this supported.

As is true for all the exercises in this book, whatever comes up for you is totally okay. We are trying to let go of shame now, so remind yourself that you do not need to put any pressure on yourself to feel a certain way, nor do you need to feel shame about what this brings up for you. This journey is about being honest with ourselves, even when it feels uncomfortable.

Exercises like this can be valuable in understanding the roots of our shame. Many people developed negative core beliefs about themselves during past experiences,

```
I received rude comments about my looks online
```

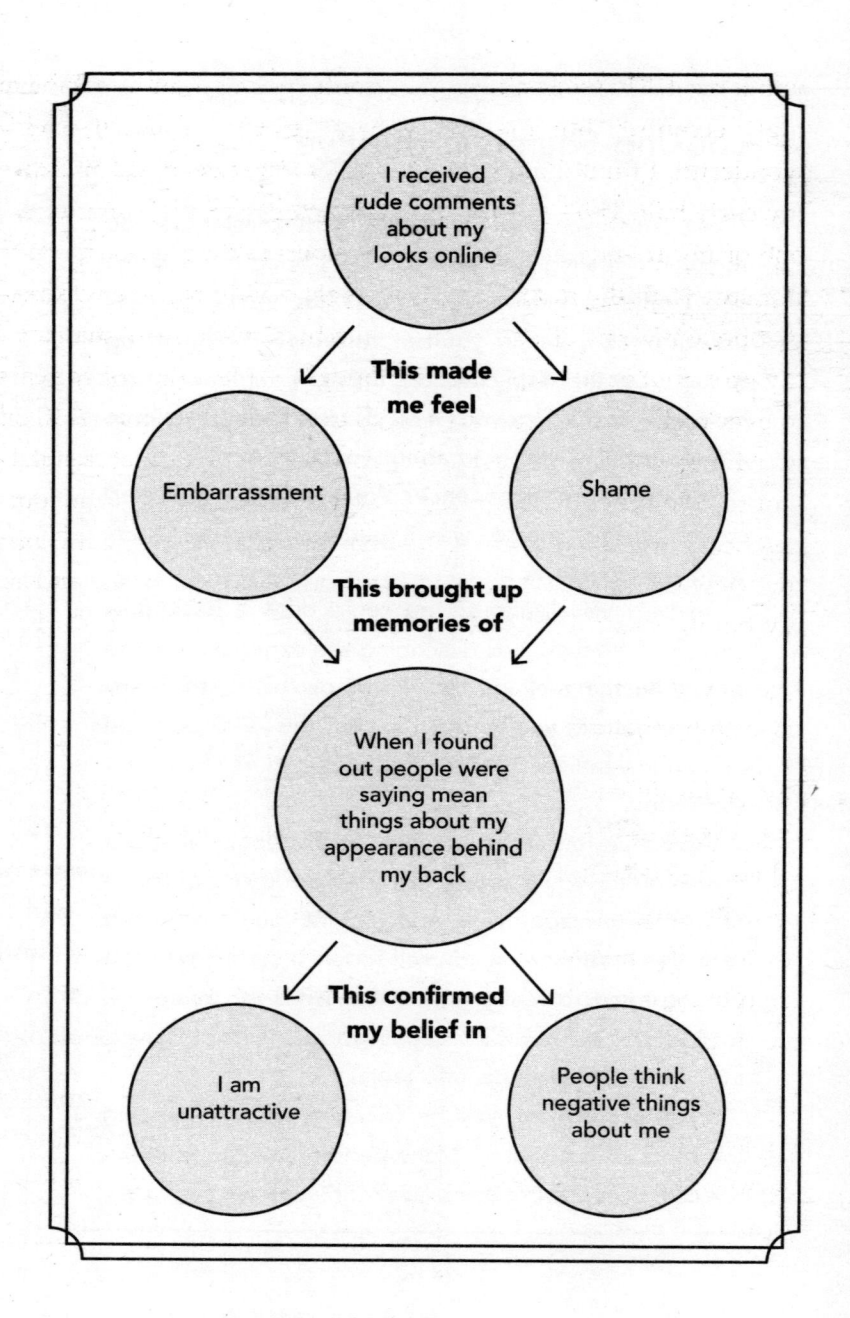

This made me feel

```
Embarrassment        Shame
```

This brought up memories of

```
When I found out people were saying mean things about my appearance behind my back
```

This confirmed my belief in

```
I am unattractive        People think negative things about me
```

which instilled feelings of shame. When shame distorts our self-perception, even new and seemingly unrelated experiences can open old wounds. We might perceive current feelings of shame as novel, unaware that new situations can trigger unresolved past shame.

You are never going to be the only person feeling or experiencing what you are – even if it seems like it, you're never alone. There are no good or bad emotions, there are only emotions and how we respond to them.

As you start to notice where shame shows up in your life, you may realize it is more prevalent around certain people. Personally, when I was really struggling with my body image, I felt a lot worse about my body when I was surrounded by people who were in smaller bodies than mine, or who I knew felt their appearance or weight to be of high importance. That wasn't their fault, but my overactive brain was in overdrive searching for unhelpful stimuli back then. If somebody else was extremely cautious about their own weight and appearance, or if they were someone who put a lot of harsh judgements on themselves, I would feel judged myself, and worry they would scrutinize my figure too.

You may also notice that you feel greater shame after scrolling on Instagram, or after consuming media which bombards you with pictures of people who meet the latest beauty standard. Noticing this is important, because it allows us to begin to separate what are our personal, real beliefs and what we have internalized from society or what has been projected onto us by others. It's not about blaming anyone around us, because many of those people are also struggling with shame around their appearances and have misplaced a sense of importance in their exterior, but it can be helpful to add a degree of separation from those people when we begin to heal. That separation, though it may sound daunting, doesn't have to look like cutting people off or avoiding friends, it can simply be asking not to talk about topics like food, diet and weight; most people will understand! There are also things you can do like deleting apps that you find negatively impact you or limiting people's posts on social media, but most of all, it's about building your foundations: knowing what you value, prioritizing your resilience and strengthening the beliefs you want to walk through life with.

When trying to unpick my shame, and differentiate learned beliefs from core values, I found it helpful to imagine somebody else with the same insecurity, and to envisage how I'd react. I put myself in the shoes of those I presumed were judging me. Let's say I felt ashamed because I had blemishes on my skin. 'If I saw a young girl with acne on her cheeks,' I asked myself, 'would I notice? And if I noticed, what would my thought process be? Would I judge her for something so irrelevant?' I lived much of my life in an extremely self-conscious state because I imagined that if I made even a quick trip to the shops without covering up my acne, everybody who walked past would notice, judge, and think horrible things about me. When I had the breakthrough realization that the majority of people are too focused on themselves to care at all or even look at you, I understood that I'd been living as though I was the centre of everybody's attention. The ultimate reality of life is that we are all at the centre of our own universe. Nobody's focused on you! And that is so freeing.

The last time I went to the shops, I likely walked past hundreds of people, but my memory is of shopping. When I last walked my dog, I'm sure we passed a dozen strangers, but I couldn't identify their faces in a crowd. And even when a person has had a noticeable physical difference, it has merely registered in my brain, and then I've moved on. When I say, 'why would anybody care about your skin?', don't take that to mean that you're self-centred – you're not. I just mean people don't *care* in the way we think they do. When insecurity dominates our minds, shame convinces us that the things we are insecure about are far more significant than they are. We imagine that our insecurities are the first thing others will notice. The reality is that nobody is looking and nobody is judging – and if they were, they'd forget within minutes. It's through fear that we imagine others' revulsion towards us, not self-absorption.

When I confronted how anxious it made me to be seen without makeup, I realized that an awful lot of my appearance-based anxieties would disappear if I never had to be perceived by others. But that is how I know these are not my core beliefs. That is what makes it obvious to me that the shame I held around my appearance was taught. It's frustrating really, because throughout history, over and over again, people have just decided what is the current 'right', most 'attractive' way to look, behave and live, regardless of whether we personally subscribe to the same ideas. If you're not consciously avoiding being influenced by trends, it's very easy to end up living by values that are not actually *your* values at all.

A big part of my journey was confronting the fact that so much of the way I had been living my life was not true to me. I realized that I was living to impress an invisible entity, living for the approval of everyone around me, who didn't really care about the parts of me I was so focused on 'fixing'. Carrying the weight of shame on your shoulders for something so insignificant to those who love you? That seems an absurd way to go through life.

I don't care what the strangers who walk past me think of me, because I can confidently say that I like who I am. And when I receive unkind comments online, as is expected with my work, I know they are projection. People are unkind because they are unhappy. I will not take their shame and make it mine. I don't care if the people around me conflate being big-headed with being confident. Part of embracing confidence and unlearning shame is realizing that confidence and cockiness are, fundamentally, not the same thing, and that confidence allows us to flourish and to thrive, but a lack of it will limit our potential.

It's okay to slip up during the unlearning process. It's okay to have days where you don't feel confident. That doesn't mean you're failing at confidence. It's easy to try to apply our perfectionism to the healing process, too, but the beautiful, and difficult, thing about healing is that it is messy. We will slip up. We will fall and get up again. What is important is that we stay strong, determined, sure in what we know – we are deserving of self-acceptance, and life will be so much richer for us and for those in our lives if we spend less time wrapped up in hating ourselves, caught in the hamster wheel chasing perfection.

How did I unlearn shame?

Knowing that the negative beliefs you carry around yourself and your appearance, and the idea of being okay with who you are, is unfounded, doesn't instantly make shame disappear. Here are some practical steps, albeit small, that helped me to let go of it.

No longer apologizing for things that weren't my fault

For a large part of my life, I have been a chronic over-apologizer. I can find ways to apologize for things that couldn't even slightly be my fault. It's impressive when I think about the mental gymnastics I used to do to manage to blame myself for things. At the crux of my excessive apologizing was shame, and shame is undoubtedly a huge contributor to many people's tendency to over-apologize. Over-apologizing is a behaviour I still sometimes find myself slipping back into, without meaning to. It's natural for our minds to slip back into behaviours we used to rely on.

Growing up, apologizing for everything I did felt safe. It felt like if I acknowledged any tiny thing I'd done and immediately apologized for it, I covered all bases, and if what I'd done had offended someone and I hadn't realized, it would be okay because I'd apologized. I also think years and years of talking down to myself led me to believe I was an inconvenience and was irritating or upsetting those around me, even when, to the average person, the situation would show no evidence of that. For context, too, I did grow up with undiagnosed ADHD, and I imagine part of my worry around not knowing if others were mad at me stemmed from my neurodivergent brain sometimes struggling to read social situations well.

When you have such a low opinion of yourself, you can end up convincing yourself your mere existence is an inconvenience. I need you to know that you are not an inconvenience. You don't owe anyone anything. You don't owe the world an apology. In Part 3: Forgive Yourself (page 145), we will talk more about the fact that humans are not infallible. But for now, in order to know it's okay to not spend your life apologizing for things you don't need to, just know this: it's okay to make mistakes. If others are angry with you, it is their responsibility to communicate that with you and let you know. Until then, unless you have very obviously physically hurt them or said something extremely unkind, you do not need to apologize. It's not your responsibility to monitor every situation and find your faults.

It is important to recognize what you want and need in situations, rather than adapting your thinking, and subsequently your actions, to keep everyone else happy. Your needs matter, too! You are not a burden for needing to do things which may inconvenience others at times, or for accepting help. You were not put on this Earth to shrink and please everybody but yourself, so stop apologizing for your existence.

Not joining in on conversations about other women being 'too confident'

Though I'm not proud of it, I have definitely engaged in gossiping before. I have definitely been guilty of calling another person 'over-confident'. And I hate that. I hate that I grew up thinking it was embarrassing to like yourself. It isn't. There is no shame in believing in yourself. And now that I know that, and believe it wholeheartedly, I refuse to engage in putting others down for embracing themselves. You'll see, as you let go of judgements against others, you'll find it a lot easier to embrace your own confidence. If you are not shaming others, you will find you shame yourself less. That being said, please do not hold guilt or shame for having judgemental thoughts. It is in our nature, as humans, and also deeply ingrained within our society. It is not your fault if you have been prone to judging others, but watch how you flourish when you unlearn that urge.

Actively saying 'I am proud of myself'

This is a fundamental step and one that we will delve into in more detail in the next chapter, but being able to feel pride in your achievements is life-changing. One thing I made certain I did regularly throughout my ED recovery and my healing journey, was to say, 'I am proud of myself'. Even if it was for something others wouldn't have been proud of themselves for, if it was a big thing for me, or just something I didn't expect myself to be able to do, I told myself I was proud of myself. I often said it aloud in the videos I was sharing online at the time, but I felt that writing it down in a journal helped to affirm it within my mind, too. You should be proud of yourself. I can guarantee that you've survived days you didn't think you would. You've gone through painful, difficult things and you've come out the other side. Here you are, reading a book to try to understand yourself more and better your headspace. I am so proud of you! Be proud of yourself, too.

Remembering what is actually important about who I am

Though it makes me so sad now, my reality used to be living with immense shame for just being myself. I felt unlikeable, not pretty enough, not funny enough, not interesting enough, and I found that when meeting new people, shame around who I was sat at the forefront of my mind. My social anxiety actually felt a lot like embarrassment. It tainted most of the interactions I had with others because I felt so inferior. I never entered conversations or spaces with confidence, instead, I wanted to shrink myself and go unnoticed altogether.

Crucially, unlearning shame also means learning to value yourself and cultivating your self-talk to focus on the many wonderful parts of you. I know as well as the next person that when you're in a negative headspace, reading positive quotes is like water off a duck's back. There is nothing less simple than the oversimplified idea of just 'being positive'. So, even if you're reading this and believing that you're the exception, that there's *nothing* good about you, I know for a fact that there is. It's so hard to let any of that positivity infiltrate when you are filled with a constant barrage of negative self-talk, but I am going to be the little cheerleader on your shoulder as you read this, reminding you that no matter what the self-doubt brain wants you to believe, there is so much good within you.

Without even meeting you, I can think of three things I know to be true about you as a reader of this book, which are undoubtedly lovely attributes:

1) **You evidently care about being kinder to yourself.** A wonderful quality, which will in turn help you to be kinder to others and walk through the world with confidence. And when your focus shifts and your brain has more energy to put elsewhere, it'll enable you to be your best self and to do things you wouldn't have previously believed you could.

2) **You have a level of self-awareness that many people don't have** – you have picked up this book because you know that you engage in unhelpful thought patterns. Self-help may be an idea that is less taboo now, and is spoken of more often, but many people still hold the mindset that they don't need to work on themselves. You are reading this and trying to better your life. That shows emotional intelligence, maturity and strength.

3) **You are strong.** You have an openness to vulnerability. Don't overlook the bravery it takes to confront negative

thoughts and to work on your mindset. This book is tackling some difficult-to-face feelings and you're taking it in your stride.

Can you see how easy it is for me to know there are wonderful things about you without ever even meeting or interacting with you? In every small action you take, there are good motivations and signs of positive attributes within you. This is why celebrating little wins is so important, but it also goes to show that when we put our entire worth into what society prioritizes, we are bound to feel shame and to believe we aren't doing enough.

As we move through life in this ever-changing, competitive and metric-driven world, it's easy to be swept up in the relentless, false importance of it all. Self-inflicted pressure is a thread that runs through many areas of life, from school exam grades, to university stress, to job promotions, to the worry around joining a new workplace, to meeting new people, to feeling you have to look a certain way.

I love my friends because they are kind, caring, emotionally intelligent, open, warm and funny. I don't remember what grades any of them received in their exams. I don't know how much any of them weigh. But most of all, I don't care, and nor does anybody else.

Look for the good in all of the places you usually wouldn't – the kindness in how you chose a gift for your friend, the compassion in how you listen when somebody needs you, the strength in how you've survived every challenge you've faced. You are more than the vessel that carries you, more than the face you put on for the world, more than what you see when you look in the mirror. More than your grades, more than your salary, more than can be measured in material possessions or numbers of any kind.

You may not believe it because you're still struggling to recognize your wonderful qualities, but that doesn't mean they're not there, it just means your negative self-talk is withholding your ability to see it! To think some people can't pinpoint a single thing they feel is good about themselves is heartbreaking, because we all have so much good inside us.

I no longer feel shame for things I once did. I have become headstrong in my beliefs about self-confidence and I've learned to let them drown out my inner critic. I know how to counter-argue now, when that voice tells me that it's embarrassing to feel good about myself or to believe I am good at things, or when it tries to stifle my joy because freedom and confidence is unknown territory. It took practice to stop cringing when I said nice things to myself, but I feel such power in my ability to speak up for myself.

When I started to feel okay telling myself I looked good, I stepped into my day with more confidence. I stopped worrying about every calorie I consumed and I trusted that by being kind to myself and my body, it would figure things out. I stopped micro-managing my interactions with others because I knew, deep down, through repeatedly telling myself so, that I deserved friends who opened their arms to every part of the person I am, that I deserved to be loved wholly.

The truth is that lots of us simply do not know how to be kind to ourselves, and may even find the concept a little bit embarrassing, but part of the journey is unlearning that shame. In the next chapter, we will cover the practical steps I implemented to make my new, kinder beliefs about myself stick. It is not boastful to be proud of yourself. It is not a crime to celebrate your wins. It is not egotistical to feel good in your body. It is a wonderful thing to know yourself, to accept yourself, to be self-assured.

Chapter 6
Proactive Changes

You are worthy of self-acceptance, always.

So far, we've spoken mostly about mindset and unpicking the origins of our negative self-talk. The real change I experienced, though, came when I began to implement tangible, proactive changes in my day-to-day life. Over many years of engaging with negative self-talk, my brain had hardwired itself into those patterns, and I had to engage in some 'opposite actions' to unpick the behaviours that were keeping my negative self-talk alive. For me, opposite actions have been a huge part of my healing, and are especially useful if you're struggling to know how to begin to make perceptible change within your own mind. Opposite actions involve dedicating yourself to doing things that feel unnatural and uncomfortable and that challenge the negative core beliefs you hold about yourself. When I wanted to cancel plans because I thought my friends hated me, I'd message to confirm what time we were meeting, so I couldn't back out. When I wanted to change my outfit at the last minute because I'd spiralled into insulting myself, I quickly left the house in the outfit. Step one is developing an awareness of your thought patterns and self-talk, step two is taking the reins.

An important thing to note: this journey is about letting go of perfection, not hyperfixating on following an immaculate healing journey. This isn't about curating a flawless mindset or *perfecting* your self-talk. Life is unpredictable, and this journey will also be unpredictable at times. Resist the urge to make snap judgements about yourself, or to bottle up any emotions when things feel overwhelming – the hardest moments often result in the greatest growth and highlight what we are still struggling with. If you find yourself, months down the line, realizing you've slipped back into a negative internal narrative, know that you haven't failed, this is just a chance to learn to recognize your triggers.

Healing from hardwired thought patterns is a process, not a switch that will happen overnight. You also should know that our brains will sometimes seek the comfort of what soothes us, of what is familiar, and that's okay. The negative beliefs we hold about ourselves are deeply ingrained and it's natural that we will have days where old ways sneak back in, but that is not a step backwards, simply a chance to practise your skills and remind yourself of why you started this journey. It is going to take time, and practice, for neutral self-talk to become second nature. When your inner critic rears its ugly head (which it will), know that this isn't your fault. You aren't doing anything wrong, nor are you hopeless or a lost cause. You are just experiencing the unavoidable ups and downs that we all will as humans. This journey is about strengthening our friendship with ourselves and changing how we react to life's unexpected lows. This journey *isn't* about snapping our fingers and being the world's most positive, healed person. It's about being one per cent kinder to yourself every day, regardless of whether we take small steps 'backwards' in the process.

And on that note, please don't give up because you aren't seeing immediate results. These habits and beliefs have hardened and set over the (likely) many years you have been engaging with them. For many of us, self-deprecation has hijacked our reflex responses and become our gut reaction. With consistency and dedication to implementing proactive changes, however, you can slowly start to chip away at the thoughts that keep you stuck and make you miserable.

My small changes

A year after I'd made the decision to dedicate myself to recovery from my eating disorder, I noticed my self-talk was slipping back into risky territory. Adjusting to life in a body that had just gone through such a drastic change and was still learning to trust me was never going to be easy, I'd known that from the start. But I hadn't expected to feel such guilt about the time I'd spent unwell.

My eyes burned patterns into the ceiling as I lay awake, white swirls swelling and fading into the dark as I blinked. I'd been spending night after night like this recently, unable to fall asleep as I listened to my brain berate me. Grieving the life I could have had was a cruel way of torturing myself, and though I knew I'd not chosen to become unwell, I blamed myself wholly. *You ruined your chance of going to university. You'll never get your teenage years back, you wasted them, you're useless. You may as well give up.* Alone in my bed, I watched my mind hurtle down a familiar track, knowing soon I'd crash hard into my old self-hateful patterns.

It felt as though somebody was lying on top of my chest. My brain was hurling insults again, constantly presenting new arguments as to why I was worthless. I pulled my duvet up over my chin, tucking myself in until I was cocooned, and closed my eyes. *I cannot do this again*, I thought to myself, my reason just a whisper. *I cannot go backwards. I know where this leads.* A tear escaped my eye and, still hugging myself with my duvet, still curled inside my cocoon, I turned over and let my pillow catch my tears.

I sighed. Fighting my brain was tiring. It was exhausting having to choose to be kind to myself every day when my brain seemed so enthusiastic about doing the opposite. And sometimes, just like on this night, when I was worn out and struggling to keep going, I'd have no choice but to accept that I'd been gradually letting myself slip.

I started my own healing journey multiple times. It was unpredictable throughout. It was far from linear. I would make huge strides, feel as though I was in such a good place and yet, out of the blue, something small would trigger my inner critic, and if I didn't catch myself in time I'd soon be falling into a negative spiral. My black-and-white thinking led me to feel as though I'd wiped all my progress in a single moment. This, naturally, was so upsetting because after months of hard work, it would feel like I was right back at square one, looking down in despair at a version of me who didn't know how to fight back. But I wasn't, this was just the nature of healing, and my habituality, my humanness, was seeking the comfort of what it knew. Actually, it was useful for me to take the low moments as an opportunity to remind myself of how far I'd come.

When these negative feelings and thoughts inevitably came up, I was reminded that I had made such immense progress to even be able to acknowledge that I wasn't talking to myself in the way I wanted to be. There once was a version of me who only knew how to be harsh and unkind to myself, and yet here I was, upset that I was behaving in that way. What a win! It's important to acknowledge your small wins along this journey – you are allowed to feel proud of your progress.

Let's pause for a moment of reflection

What is one thing you're proud of yourself for this week? It can be as small as getting out of bed on a hard day, or as big as passing an exam. For example, as I'm writing this, I'd say my biggest win this week is that I left an event early when I was feeling panicked. To some that may seem like a failure, but it's progress for me to acknowledge my needs and leave situations that are making me feel worse.

All wins are worthy wins, and learning to celebrate ourselves is a fundamental part of this journey to self-acceptance.

A belief that people often hold, which causes them to push away the idea of healing their relationship with themselves altogether, is not feeling 'bad' enough to need to heal. It's so easy to convince ourselves we're being dramatic. As someone prone to minimizing my own issues out of fear that I'm being dramatic, I understand the thought process that comes with it. There will always be someone who you feel is worse off than you, someone who you perceive to be struggling more. In a world where extreme and tragic stories are broadcast to us on a day-to-day basis, it's easy to feel our struggles are minimal in comparison. And in truth, maybe there are worse things happening in the world. There are, sadly, always going to be horrific events happening to others around the world. But everything is relative, and this is *your* life. You are the one who has to wake up each day and live inside a mind filled with self-deprecating thoughts, and you are not dramatic for struggling with that. Denying your problems achieves nothing; it doesn't make other problems in the world better, it only withholds the self-compassion you need in order to heal. You wouldn't tell a friend that their problems don't matter, so don't say it to yourself.

Let's not overlook the fact that prioritizing self-care can actually be a force for good, too. Healing my relationship with myself and my body has actually enabled me to put more good out into the world. When I was wrapped up in self-hatred, I spent so much of my time trying to 'fix' things about myself that didn't need fixing, and now I have both more time and more mental space to focus on helping others.

Worrying that you are not 'bad' enough to start to be kinder to yourself is evidence itself of what's wrong – the belief that any level of self-hatred is okay. Many of us have a deep-seated belief that we are not worthy of kindness, or that being kind to ourselves isn't a priority. The truth is, denying yourself the act of healing is a vicious cycle. You'll feel miserable, and then you'll acknowledge the fact that your mind is not a nice place to be. You'll get down about that and think about trying to work on it but then decide that, actually, your life isn't bad enough to need to implement change. You fixate on the idea that others have it worse, that you're being dramatic, and the cycle starts again.

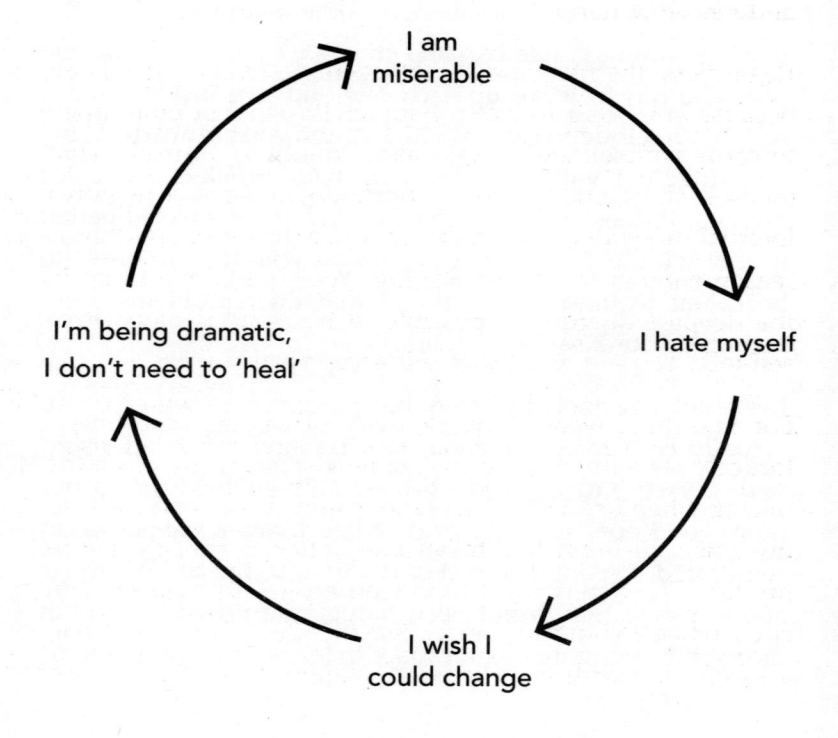

I am miserable → I hate myself → I wish I could change → I'm being dramatic, I don't need to 'heal' → (repeats)

Having been through the mental health system, having known many others who have been through it also and having witnessed how differently each individual mind responds to the approaches used to treat mental health struggles, I am acutely aware that the same approach will not work for everyone. For anyone who still finds themselves wrapped up in this cycle while reading this book, it may be less intimidating if you don't label this as a 'journey' but instead just take what you need from each part of this book. Choosing to work on your sense of self doesn't have to be a big, scary, labelled event. It can be as simple as saying, 'I'm going to make a little more effort to be kinder to myself and see what happens'.

Regardless, the likelihood is that you are reading this book because you want to live a happier life, to feel more open towards yourself and to talk more kindly to yourself. That in itself shows that there is, deep down, both a negative internal monologue and a desire to feel happier, and that is reason enough to choose healing. You don't have to be in the deepest depression possible to be in need of positive self-talk. You are worthy of self-acceptance, always.

For me, there were many catalysts of change. The time I locked eyes with an unrecognizable version of myself in the mirror, when I saw grey skin and thinning hair and realized my eating disorder had taken away almost all of the joy in my life. The time I went to put on my favourite jeans and cried when I could no longer zip them up. The time I had a lovely day with my friends but upon coming home just curled up in bed and worried all night that they secretly hated me. They were not all 'extreme' situations, but they each were points where I noticed my negative self-talk was making me miserable, and eventually I got so sick of the vitriol that I vowed to change it.

That's really all you need to start this journey – an awareness that the way you talk to yourself is affecting your life, and a willingness to change.

So, what proactive changes did I make?

Throughout my journey there have been some habits I built that made a real, tangible difference in my life. I would also like to add in a little disclaimer here: I am not a medical professional, and it is important to seek professional help if/when you feel you need it. This book and the exercises I share within it will hopefully be a helpful guide towards self-acceptance, but I am quite aware it cannot be a cure for mental illness, nor replace therapy. Please know that you are deserving of seeking help for your struggles, and there is nothing to be embarrassed about if you do.

There were many small ways in which I brought self-compassion and self-care into my daily life. Some I learned through my time in therapy, some I stumbled into while trying to tackle things myself. It did, at times, feel quite exhausting to be constantly attuned to my thoughts, but I had to be in order to tackle each negative belief that I held. Part of me found it all tedious, the little bit in my brain that told me I was silly for trying to be kind to myself. Naturally, though, it became much less tiring when I got used to engaging in these practices. They started to feel a little less foreign and, in time, I began to reap their benefits.

When you try out some of these exercises and activities, you might at first feel a little silly. I know I did! Remember that if it helps, it helps, and it's worth trying, even if it's a little off-piste. Beginning to engage in opposite behaviours to those we are used to relying on, understandably, might feel foreign and uncomfortable, but we have to move past the discomfort in order for these practices to become second nature. Allow yourself to feel whatever comes up for you, without judgement. This isn't about labelling thoughts and feelings as good or bad, but about observing them and learning from them.

1. Covering my mirror

Sometimes we stay in spaces that are harming us because we are used to them. Many anxious people feel soothed by knowing exactly what is coming, so remaining in familiar, painful situations can feel preferable when the other option is to face the unknown. When paying close attention to my internal monologue, I became acutely aware that it was at its loudest and most negative when I was standing in front of my full-length mirror. I couldn't walk past it without just taking a quick look, which then turned into full-on scrutiny of every part of my body. If that was how I started my day (it was, every day), my brain would be filled with self-deprecating thoughts from the get-go, and those thoughts then fed off each other and grew bigger, running rampant around my brain for the rest of the day.

Covering my mirror, however, broke the habitual nature of my appearance-related negative self-talk. This was a somewhat drastic move for me, as somebody who used to obsessively check how my body looked throughout the day. Ironically, scrutinizing my body in the mirror was a very comforting pastime for me, so it felt incredibly anxiety-provoking at first to not have that behaviour to fall back on. The terror of my body changing, or of developing a new spot, or of me looking 'ugly' and not knowing, was paralysing. But over time new habits formed, and I got used to not inspecting every inch of my skin. I soon learned that nothing actually changed if I wasn't aware of how every part of me looked, other than the fact that the unkind voice in my mind got a little quieter.

While I needed a mirror to be able to see if my outfit looked okay, I knew I also needed a barrier between me and this evident trigger for my inner critic, and so I did just that. I made my triggering behaviour less accessible and I covered my mirror with a stick-on blind, cut to fit. For people with appearance-related anxieties, this exercise can be tough, but it is extremely helpful. You don't have to buy anything new or fancy – you can use sheets of paper, an old curtain, a blanket, a temporary roll-up blind – just cover the mirror(s) that you find yourself obsessing over flaws in most.

To be realistic, I allowed myself a timed two minutes of

mirror time each morning to check my outfit, hair and makeup. It's okay to check for actual issues (like the fact you were about to leave the house in your slippers – been there, done that), but be as objective as possible. Check your outfit matches, make sure there isn't mascara smudged across your nose, but then walk away the second your inner critic pipes up. In the next chapter we will cover how to talk back in the moments that it does, but for now, create the initial barrier and tackle the reliance on appearance-checking.

2. Unfollow, unfollow, unfollow

It may be a cliché, but it's true: comparison *is* the thief of joy. And, as we spoke about in Chapter 3, social media is a breeding ground for it. Something that I found beneficial as I started to work on my self-image was unfollowing literally *anybody* who made me feel worse about myself. I began to monitor how I felt as I scrolled my Instagram feed, and if any content I consumed slightly triggered me, I'd hit unfollow. Those I found to be negatively impacting me weren't actually doing anything malicious or wrong, they were simply sharing their lives online. But it felt like being bombarded by others who were skinnier than me, had clearer skin, or had seemingly perfect lives, and this only amplified the negative voice already living in my head.

Though I always rolled my eyes when, as a teen, my parents told me how bad my phone was for me, they had a point. So many of us habitually reach for our phones to fill any idle minute. To be spending such a large chunk of our spare time inside a picture-perfect curated world can really skew our perception of what is 'normal'. Next time you use social media, make an effort to notice your thoughts and how they change as you scroll. Be conscious of any content that leaves you feeling you need to alter yourself in some way, and continue to check in with yourself. Ask yourself: *Are any of these posts bringing up negative emotions for me? Is consuming this content increasing the unkind thoughts I have about myself?* If your response is yes, unfollow.

Even if you enjoy the content created by the person posting, continuing to follow somebody who triggers your negative self-talk in any way is making your timeline a potentially harmful place. Know that it's okay to put boundaries in, it's okay to not want to see a person's content. It's not rude, it's self-preservation. We, as humans, were not built to know what everyone else is doing all of the time, or to be able to easily access such comparable metrics that directly link to approval around our appearances.

There were times when I unfollowed people I knew in real life, mostly others who struggled with an eating disorder and who triggered my body image issues. Sometimes they did notice and ask me what they'd done wrong, to which I responded that it was entirely a me problem. They'd done nothing wrong, I was simply in a vulnerable place and was making sure my timeline didn't have any content that caused my brain to compare. They never minded and the response was always one of understanding. People are kinder than I expect, as somebody with an anxious brain. However, if unfollowing feels too cutthroat or puts you more on edge, see if the app you're using offers a 'mute' option. What matters is that you see less of the content you're comparing yourself to. Sometimes, what feels like mindless scrolling is actually giving your brain new information to torment you with, and it's easy to forget that social media is a highlight reel, not reality.

3. Create a bank of distractions for times when you start to feel you're spiralling

Facing our self-hateful ruminations head on is a necessary step towards healing. There are, however, times when using distractions to stop negative thought spirals escalating is the best way forward. If you can, create a bank of distractions that take your mind away from the intensity of your thoughts in that moment. You could do this by building yourself a 'distraction box' and putting physical distractions inside it so it's quick to grab and use, or making a list of activities you know you enjoy that aren't on your phone. Try to make them engaging, unrelated to social media and separate from anything to do with your appearance. By unrelated to your appearance, I mean that even if things like clothes shopping seem like a good idea (I definitely had a bit of a retail therapy phase when I was struggling), being confronted by models' bodies and dealing with size guides can make you feel worse.

If you, like me, struggle with staying focused on one thing at a time, putting on your favourite playlist or a comfort TV show in the background while you play a game, journal, doodle or go on a walk can be the sweet spot.

Some distraction box ideas
- Colouring books.
- Crocheting/knitting.
- A notebook.
- Jigsaw puzzles.
- Fidget toys.
- Word searches/word puzzles.
- Headphones, to listen to music or a podcast.
- A cuddly toy/comfort item.

Some activity list ideas
- Put on your favourite show.
- Go on a walk in nature.
- Do arts and crafts that you enjoy.
- Avoid being alone: chat with someone you love.
- Play a board game.
- Tidy your room/home.
- Make birthday or Christmas cards.
- Read a book.

4. Flip the negatives

I'm not going to pretend it's easy to say nice things to yourself when you don't believe them. It's not. It feels icky, wrong, and for some of us it can be hard to even think of things we like about ourselves. This will change as the journey progresses, but I know I wanted to scream in the face of anyone who asked me to say nice things to myself when I was in a dark headspace. Every emotion that comes up for you when you try these is welcomed. It's okay to find it awkward at first. Just do your best to stick with it, because putting your mental health first is never silly.

As I said, it will get easier, but for now I want you to focus on directly flipping the thoughts you're currently having about yourself. It may sound strange, but that was the only way I learned to be able to say nice things about myself. I decided that every time I had a nasty thought about myself, I would respond with the exact opposite of that thought. This added some nuance into my mindset. I found this a good starting point as you don't need to think really deeply or focus on things you like about yourself – I know that's not an easy feat. To start with, either aloud or in your mind, say the direct opposite of whichever negative thought has come up for you. You don't have to believe what you're saying yet, just trust the process!

For example:
I look so ugly.
I do not look ugly.

I am so annoying.
I am not annoying.

My spots make me unattractive.
My spots do not make me unattractive.

I wish my thighs were smaller.
My thighs are okay as they are.

My friends hate me.
My friends do not hate me.

What you say doesn't need to be intimidatingly positive, it just needs to be a statement. It's like subliminal messaging to your inner critic – it will eventually get the hint that it doesn't control you, and it will also be given new, opposing information to challenge its narrative.

Again, you don't have to believe what you're saying at first; it's okay, that bit will take time. Just know that you're stepping closer to a life where you feel neutral towards yourself, a life where you can make it through the day without persistent critical thoughts. If you're currently struggling to see a way out, like I was when I embarked on this journey, I want to quickly remind you that there is a life where these thoughts are not at the forefront of your mind all day. I didn't think it was possible, but it is. There is a version of you who gets there, too.

In time, turning the tables on your reflexive negative self-talk will start to feel more comfortable, and a little less alien, and you can try to talk *kindly* to yourself. If you feel overwhelmed at any point on this journey, remember: this is *your* journey, to be taken at a pace you can handle, and any small changes or activities that help you, whether they're mentioned here or not, are going to get you to a freer, happier life.

In the next chapter, we'll go through some ways that you can put positive self-talk into action.

Chapter 7
Talking Back

You are still learning, and always will be.

I have always been the sort of person who will avoid uncomfortable experiences at all costs. The sweat collecting in my palms when I know I have to face adulthood and, with shaking hands, make a phone call. The tightness in my chest that comes with meeting new people by myself. The anxiety of the dentist, the doctors, difficult conversations, the unknown. I'm a creature of habit, of comfort. I'd much rather stay in the safety of what I know than push myself out of my comfort zone. I know I'm not alone in that either. It is a very human way to feel.

My comfort zone, however, became a miserable place for me to exist in. Avoiding discomfort meant my life ended up very small. I relied on my mum to make my phone calls for me,

I couldn't wear clothes that clung to my skin for fear of my body being seen, I didn't ever meet new people or have new experiences. I didn't trust the outside world. I was trapped in a bubble with only my inner critic and my anxiety, and after a while I felt totally suffocated.

There were many different steps that I took to break out of that bubble, but an important one was learning to do the most uncomfortable thing I could within my own mind – to talk back to my inner critic.

During the two minutes of my morning that I'd designated as 'mirror time', my negative self-talk ran rampant. I went into overdrive. In a whirlwind of insults and ensuing panic, those familiar feelings would surface, and I'd feel urged to hide myself away again. As my body physically was changing during the time I was going through this journey, it was as though my brain wanted to cram hours of scrutiny into the two minutes I'd given myself. In the interest of transparency, there were times when I was stuck in front of my mirror for much longer than two minutes. As you will repeatedly hear me say – there is no way to heal perfectly. This journey will be a messy one. That is okay!

Stepping back from my reflection felt a lot like giving up a comfort blanket, because looking in the mirror was a very reassuring behaviour for me. It's an action that is very common amongst people with body image issues, often referred to as 'body checking'. During this journey, I was regaining the weight I'd lost due to my eating disorder, and body checking was definitely something I struggled with. It is my belief that more of us engage in forms of this habit than we realize. Appearance-related anxiety means a lot of us do feel a sense of comfort from being able to check our appearance, whether that shows up as looking at our reflection multiple times before leaving the house, glancing at a pocket mirror often, or regularly opening our front cameras on our phones to see how we look.

In the beginning, trying to counteract my own thoughts was so difficult. I was having arguments with myself. Talking back to my inner critic brought up the exact uncomfortable feeling I usually ran from. It could be quite a draining experience at times, and I just wanted to sit back and leave it be, as I had for so long. Every day I had to choose to work towards an unknown, unfamiliar way of being and to step out of my comfort zone. Fighting back felt like so much effort, despite the fact that all the action was happening in my head, invisible to others. However, the more you do it, the less strange and the more comfortable it starts to feel. It wasn't long before it started to energize me more than it drained me. In those moments, where I stood in front of the mirror in my childhood bedroom and first found my voice, I could feel a change within me.

To overcome the intense attachment and value I had put upon my exterior, I had to learn that my appearance didn't define me. It wasn't what people cared about when they looked at me. I didn't judge anyone else's appearance in the way I judged myself, so nobody was going to look at me and analyse mine. Staring into the mirror all the time didn't change how my body looked, and actually it was okay if my hair was a bit of a mess sometimes, or if my mascara was slightly smudged. Letting go of devotedly checking myself in the mirror also signified letting go of perfection, letting go of my need to control my body and my appearance, and letting go of obsessive scrutiny.

Having spent years being trampled by my own negative self-perception, using my voice and offering myself a new perspective was both alien and exciting. Back then, I felt so small, my inner critic so large and looming that it towered over me. To begin with, opposing the beliefs I had clung to for so long felt as though I were a naughty child, as if I was talking out of turn, speaking without being asked to. There was a beauty in connecting with that childlike version of myself, though, because some of the beliefs I was carrying had formed early in childhood.

Your inner child

Throughout my time in therapy, I have learned about the importance of giving your inner child care and attention. 'Inner child' has become a popularly used term on social media, but it's not just a trend, it's a well-studied concept. In analytical psychology it is said that the inner child is a part of your subconscious mind that has been absorbing information from the world around you since you were very young. It is the part of you that holds onto emotions, memories and beliefs from your early years, as well as the hope and excitement you had for the future. It can also be triggered by experiences that bring up emotional parallels to those you struggled with during childhood. Our inner child lives within us, no matter what age we are.

A helpful exercise could be to stick a picture of yourself as a child on your mirror. That way, every time you are looking in the mirror and begin to say negative things to yourself, it can serve as a reminder that you are also saying those things to the versions of you who have come before. Those versions of you have built the person you are today and the way you speak to yourself right now is building future you, too. Would you criticize your childhood self, knowing that you were an innocent child, trying your best to navigate life? If not, why are you saying these things to yourself now? You are still allowed to make mistakes, to do things you regret – you are still learning, and always will be.

The concept of the inner child can be a little difficult to connect with for people who may hold negative feelings about their childhood self, and if this is you, that's okay. You may find it helpful to look at those childhood pictures of yourself and try to find some compassion for the younger you. These can serve as a visual reminder that you were *just a child*. Any mistakes you feel you made, or any actions you regret, were those of a child – an innocent child, still learning and growing up in a world that can be extremely unkind.

Connecting with our inner child can allow us to revisit a level of freedom, unbridled joy and excitement about things that we are encouraged to grow out of. It can also teach us a lot about why we, as adults, still struggle with things. Sometimes it is our inner child who is holding onto worries and anxieties formed early in life.

My inner child held a lot of my worries about the world being unsafe. As a young girl, I kept my anxiety to myself, and that never gave my child self the reassurance she needed to move through the world with confidence. I also, though I didn't realize it for a long time, had been quite insecure about my appearance as a child, not so much about my body but about the fact I didn't look very 'feminine'. I had a mop of wild, blonde curls that only grew outwards. I came to expect the question 'are you a boy or a girl?' from any new child on the playground and I hated that I didn't look like the other girls. I leaned into my 'tomboy-ish' side because I didn't know what else to do. My inner child held tightly onto her worries about looking different, and as I got older, they morphed into a desperation to dress and look like everyone else.

The childhood version of me was one who had been bullied repeatedly by other children at school and who had such low self-esteem that I felt I deserved it. In talking back to the negativity that ran rife within me as an adult, at last my inner child was learning that standing up for yourself is allowed. The decision to talk more kindly to myself was a decision to hold the hand of that hurt, confused version of me and to speak up for us both. I used my adult voice, for her, as well as me. I allowed myself to talk back, to believe I deserved more than to be beaten down.

Flipping the narrative

Gradually, talking back became an empowering experience. I felt a strength grow within me when I became able to flip the narrative. I flourished as my internal monologue started to reflect my new way of interacting with it.

You may be familiar with the idea that if another person stands up to a bully, the bully may give up and pipe down. Similar logic can be applied to your inner critic. You need to become the person who stands up to the bully. Eventually, the voice of your inner critic will learn that it will always be challenged, that what it says no longer goes and it'll get less confident, its insults less frequent. In time, that nasty voice in your head will become quieter.

As time went on, I became able to not just directly contrast my thoughts but flip the narrative entirely.

When I stood in front of the mirror, or when I saw a picture of myself, my thoughts still jumped to unkind places, but I could separate myself from the voice in my head. After practising 'opposite thoughts' for a while, I was able to build on them. Though I remained neutral, I could draw from my bank of new beliefs that I was forming about myself and the world, and use those to shut down my negative thoughts.

I look ugly became *I am so much more than my appearance.*

I am fat became *humans need body fat to survive. I have a body, I am not my body. I have fat, I am not fat.*

I hate my body became *I promise to accept my body in every season of life.*

Once I'd stopped squirming in my skin every time I tried to say something neutral to myself, once it had become almost second nature to talk back, I set a rule for myself. The rule was that every time I said something negative to myself, something unkind, something that I wouldn't say to a friend in my position, I had to say three nice things to myself. This, of course, was a big step, having found neutrality so difficult at first, but it really worked in constantly affirming that there was good within me.

On darker days, it wasn't an easy task to pull from my positive self-belief bank, but I tried to be strict with myself. There was real power in making an effort to be kind to myself, even on the days when I barely believed what I was saying, because it kept me connected to positive self-talk and the mindset I wanted to live in. I also told the people closest to me that I had this rule, and sometimes they'd catch me being hard on myself before I had, prompting me to stick to my promise.

Actually figuring out what is neutral self-talk and what is negative self-talk can be a bit tricky when you're so accustomed to negativity. When a thought came up for me like,

I'm being so lazy today, or, *my skin is so bad,* sometimes it would feel hard to distinguish whether that was an unkind thought or a factual thought. Am I insulting myself for no reason, or am I just acknowledging my breakout? Am I labelling resting as laziness, or should I be doing more? For thoughts like that, I would first search for any sign of negativity in the language I was using towards myself, such as 'bad' or 'lazy'. Though it is true there are times when I lack motivation to do things that would be good for me, I don't need to use a word as harsh as laziness. I can meet myself with more understanding and reframe it as a struggle with motivation.

When it came to labelling aspects of my appearance as 'bad', I had to remember the importance of neutral language. My skin is just skin – not bad, not good, just a part of me. I can describe it as inflamed, and sore, and itchy, and a multitude of unpleasant sensations, but I will not use language to insult myself. I'd also ask myself this: *is there actually anything I can do to change this issue today?* And I would know that if it wasn't something I would be able to resolve in the imminent future, I needed to make peace with it.

Another good question to keep on asking yourself when unkind thoughts come in is, *would I say this to my friend?*, or, *if a loved one said this to themselves, would I agree?*

Talk to yourself as you would talk to a friend. You are deserving of respect, care and kindness, both from those around you and from yourself. You are going to be doing life alongside yourself forever; make yourself a friend, a motivator, a cheerleader. You deserve better than to be stuck with somebody who only ever puts you down.

You deserve to receive the same love you give to others, even if you find it difficult to believe right now. In the next chapter, we will cover the process of making positive self-talk a reflex response, but for now I'd just like to take a moment to say this: you are doing so well. You have survived every single one of your worst days. I am proud of you, and you should be proud of yourself, too.

So, next time your negative self-talk says: *I am unloveable*, I want you to say: *No, I deserve to feel loved, by others and by myself.*

Chapter 8
Making Acceptance Second Nature

Hold on to hope.

As I write this, I scan back through my day. It's been an uneventful Saturday. I've had a migraine and I've felt unwell. I woke up later than my alarms were set for, and as I rolled out of bed and walked to the bathroom, my thoughts were of what I would eat for breakfast, with a bonus moment to notice the fact that I felt quite groggy. As I slipped my retainers out and washed them under the tap, I glanced into the mirror, and staring hazily back at me was the dishevelled, messy-haired girl that I am often met with in the mornings. No thoughts about my appearance registered. I placed my retainers back in their trays and headed downstairs. My morning continued as usual, with a sizeable bowl of cereal, my morning medication and a little life admin. Only later, when I am sitting in front of the mirror on the floor in my bedroom, prepping my skin for my daily makeup, do I notice

I have grown three new spots overnight. I lean into my reflection and contort my face to get a better look. Two are small little pimples. The other is really quite inflamed – a shiny, roaring red mass that juts out of my chin. *Three new spots. That's annoying.*

This is a sign of huge progress. The opinions I formed, the thoughts I had as I went throughout my morning, were not those of self-criticism. I did not feel shame, I did not put myself down. Every thought about my appearance that popped into my head had a totally neutral undertone. If I think too much about the simplicity of it all, of how forgiving my wiring is now, I start to get a little teary. Because there was a past version of me who inspected every inch of my skin as soon as I could get to a mirror in the morning. And if I'd have sprouted three new little friends on my face in the past, an onslaught of self-loathing would have ensued. I'd have been *so* upset. I'd have immediately called myself ugly, or gross, or one of the unkind words I so often threw at myself. I'd have spiralled into thoughts of how everyone had clear skin but me, of how I'd never be loveable when my skin looked so red and 'disgusting'. And then I'd have rushed back to my room to do my makeup for the day, mortified at the idea of anybody, stranger or loved one, seeing how hideous my skin was.

And yet, it didn't even occur to me today that I looked 'bad' or 'ugly', or that my spots made me unattractive. I just saw them as spots. My skin, just skin. My opinion of myself is now so neutral that thoughts of that nature don't even crop up.

This is to say that there is hope. I don't need to promise you that one day you'll have clear skin and everything will feel okay, because your skin, your body or your appearance is not the problem and it never was. I'm just going to promise you that, by working on how you talk to yourself, one day, even if your skin is erupting, your jeans no longer fit, or your body has changed in ways that in the past would have upset you – everything will still feel okay. There will be a day where acceptance becomes second nature.

As you begin this journey, it may be hard to grasp that this new way of thinking will ever feel anything but awkward and clunky and forced. I thought that too. I hope my ordinary Saturday morning can give you a glimmer of what could be. Hold on to hope.

Picking yourself up

Right now, you are a baby learning to walk. You are, as I was in the beginning stages of this journey, finding your feet and starting to stumble. You are taking a few steps and likely falling back down. I, too, fell back down many times. Just when I was becoming more confident on my feet, life tripped me up. I remember dropping out of college and spiralling into a panic about what I was going to do with my life, convinced I was useless, a failure. I cried to my mum because I was scared; I thought these thoughts were part of my past. But like babies do, you have to keep on keeping on. You'll get back up and try again. You'll take those stompy steps and with each attempt, the skill will stick a little more. When you think you've mastered walking, you'll fall down hard and the impact will send a jolt through you. Don't focus on the fact that you fell, focus on how those trips and falls have become less and less frequent. Your body and your brain will learn. One foot in front of the other, you'll keep going. It'll become muscle memory. Before you know it, you'll be running.

You are going to have to fall and pick yourself back up a hundred times before this will feel natural. Training your brain out of what might be lifelong habits is no quick task. But the key in all of this is that though healing is not a straight line, it is an upwards trajectory. Even the moments when you slip back do not discredit the progress you are making. You are still further ahead than you have ever been before, just by trying. You don't have to be perfect anymore, you just need to be better at being kind to yourself.

Consistency is key, and perhaps the most important factor in successfully building a habit. You can only control your reactions to thoughts, you cannot stop the thoughts from coming up. As we've talked about, they will persist for a while. Keeping consistency in your responses is vital. Our brains fall back on what they know, so it's about keeping up with the practices you've implemented and teaching yourself a new normal. When my brain says, *everybody thinks you're ugly*, that could easily spiral into *I'm unloveable, and my hair looks bad, and I need to change my body, and I wish I'd worn something different, and I'm anxious, and I hate the way I look.*

And that's when the floodgates open. However, when I take control and quickly respond, even just with something short and sharp like, *I'm in a thought spiral,* or, *my thoughts aren't facts,* I am nipping that spiral in the bud. Stop it before it starts. Keep your counter arguments simple and strong and know that what you're saying is true. Nobody deserves to be unkind to themselves. Nobody deserves to live with a bully in their brain. You are no exception.

As I've been writing this book, I've been thinking about the fact that the term self-love has become so intertwined with bodies and appearances. So much so that we often forget there are so many ways to show ourselves kindness without having to bring our exterior into the equation at all. Regularly engaging in self-care is one of the best ways to build a friendship with ourselves.

Self-love feels scary because the image it conjures is one of sitting in front of your reflection and saying, 'I love myself'. But self-love is so much more than how we feel about our appearances. It's acknowledging our needs, prioritizing small acts of self-care that seem unimportant but make us feel good when we engage with them. It's cooking yourself a wholesome meal and it's eating regularly. It's allowing your body to rest without judgement. It's partaking in a form of exercise you enjoy, not to punish your body, merely for enjoyment and to get your endorphins flowing. Being kind to yourself is in all of the practical ways you interact with yourself and on this journey, it will help you to follow the exercises I've written about. Alongside that, in your wider life, make time to treat yourself as a friend. Take yourself to a café, enjoy your own company, learn to be okay spending time with yourself. Doing things just because you enjoy them is a worthy use of your time. Doing what makes you happy isn't unproductive. Rest is productive in equal measure, because, as we will come onto in Chapter 12 (page 187), it is more 'productive' in the long run to allow your body the rest it needs and deserves; run-down bodies have much higher chances of stress-induced illness or injury.

To avoid unintentionally championing the ideals of toxic productivity culture, let me remind you of one thing: you don't owe the world constant productivity. I so rarely hear 'it's normal to stay in your pyjamas all day sometimes'. Or 'it's okay if you hate running'. Or 'you're not a mess because you struggle to keep your bedroom tidy'. These are all true statements, in the same way that 'getting sunlight in the morning is good for you' or 'lowering your screen time will improve your mental health' are. Yes, productivity can help us live a happy life, but prioritizing it above all else will not. Every day will not look like the 'productive day in the life' videos you see online, and that is okay. Productivity is only beneficial if you don't turn to self-criticism in the absence of it.

In Part 1 we discussed the art of noticing, specifically noticing your thoughts and the patterns they follow, your insecurities and their origins, and the core beliefs that have shaped your world. When it comes to habituating positive self-talk, continuing to monitor your thoughts and making an effort to keep noticing will hugely help. This can look like many things.

Perhaps to become more connected with yourself, it might be important for you to slow down, to practise mindfulness and notice what comes up for you when you experience certain triggers. Noticing could also mean dedicating a time each evening to check in with yourself, to take heed of anything that you felt down about during the day, or any peaks you noticed in negative self-talk. Life can get busy, and when it does, self-care can be the first thing to slip. It's easy to feel like self-care isn't a necessary or productive use of time when things feel frantic and rushed, but it is. As humans we have basic needs, one of them being attention. See being kind to yourself as a basic need – giving yourself attention and listening to the parts of you that are hurting is not a waste of time. Creating a routine of regular check-ins with yourself will allow you to notice when your thoughts are slipping into being harsher on yourself and can be a good reminder to cut yourself some slack.

On that note, let's check in. How are you doing? I know that facing up to negative self-talk can be a tiring process and can bring up a lot of raw emotions, especially when delving into where your negative beliefs stem from. This is a checkpoint to make sure you do something nice for yourself today, something that soothes you. Grab your favourite sweet treat, follow a guided meditation, run a nice bubble bath, or perhaps use the journal prompts below to centre yourself.

Journal prompts to try

- What is one thing you've achieved this week? (This can be big or small!)
- How did that achievement make you feel about yourself?
- What have you struggled with this week?
- If somebody else was struggling with what I'm struggling with right now, what would I tell them?
- Can I apply that to myself, to try to talk to myself as more of a friend?

There is also great importance in the act of trusting yourself. A hugely impactful part of self-confidence is having confidence in our own beliefs and opinions and being able to make decisions for ourselves. This is something that actually, as I write this, feels very relevant to me.

It's only in the past year that I'd say I've really learnt to trust myself. To trust my intuition, my gut, my capability and the belief that I am able to make the right decisions. I noticed, during a pretty turbulent episode in my life, that I had a really hard time trusting my own opinions. I struggled with allowing myself to make decisions without second-guessing them and wanting the validation of others. So often I have noticed myself seeking reassurance from those around me that what I believed, thought or wanted in life was 'right'. This may seem like a minor issue, and in the grand scheme of things, it's not abnormal to seek a second opinion when making big life decisions, or when entering an unfamiliar situation. But for me, my inability to trust myself and allow myself to make my own decisions without others validating them, signified a lack of trust within myself. It showed a big flaw in my self-confidence – the fact that actually, though I was a perfectly capable and knowledgeable human, I was lacking in my self-belief. I didn't see my own wants, needs and beliefs as good enough – I needed others to back them up.

Self-confidence is so much more than being able to say, 'I like my body', or, 'I look good today'. It's also being able to say, 'I trust that I can make the right decisions for myself and for my life', and 'I am capable and clever and I feel what I feel for a reason'.

For many reasons, the term self-confidence sits much more comfortably with me and my idea of healing than 'self-love'. I'm not at all against loving yourself, of course, but in my own experience, self-love felt unattainable. Having been absorbed in my self-hatred for so long, when the goal was self-love, any small, positive shifts I could have made were vetoed by my rigid mindset. I couldn't imagine a world where I woke up and said, 'I love myself'. But when I shifted the goal posts from love to neutrality, to self-acceptance and, with that, self-confidence, it felt more achievable. If self-love has always felt implausible, know that there is equal value in self-acceptance, and you can make this a world in which you feel entirely neutral towards yourself. You are allowed to use whichever phrase works for you and feels most aligned to your journey. You are working towards a life in which you trust yourself and your decisions, and in which you know the importance of acknowledging your own feelings and opinions, first and foremost. A world in which you believe in the good within you. That is self-confidence.

A lot of the time I'd find myself wondering whether my feelings were valid. I'd say things like 'am I overreacting by feeling this way?' I'd constantly question whether I was too much, too sensitive, too emotional. It's something that has changed a lot within me in recent years, and, truthfully, it's something I am still working on. When I was flat-hunting for the first time, alone, recently, I found myself asking my friend if I was 'being silly for liking it so much' about a flat I'd fallen in love with. She simply replied, 'do *you* love it?', to which I responded, 'yes'. She asked, 'does it have any flaws which really worry you?', and I said, 'yes, the location is a bit inconvenient, but apart from that I love it.'

'Can you imagine yourself living there?'

'Absolutely.'

'Well, there you go then, you've considered the issues and you still love it. It doesn't matter what I think about it.' She showed me that the answer was already within me.

Instead of verbally reassuring me, she, unbeknownst to me at the time, taught me to seek reassurance from myself. I love her for that. I didn't realize how much I struggled to trust my own opinions, and to believe that I wasn't silly or getting carried away when I felt strong emotions about something.

Walking through the world with self-belief and an inner trust, knowing that you are able to think, fend and make decisions for yourself, is a key part of self-confidence. Making acceptance second nature means embracing all aspects of you. It's trusting yourself as much as it is letting go of judging yourself. The knowledge that you are deserving of good things and positive self-talk comes hand in hand with genuinely valuing your own opinions, and believing that you can make decisions for your life, yourself. You are the person who knows you best – your closest friend, the only person who has been with you every second of every day – you are capable and strong and able to take control of your life. You just have to trust that this is true.

During this journey, and actually throughout life, you need to know that it's completely okay to need to lean on others. This is me telling you, unequivocally, that you are allowed to rely on others to hold you up sometimes. You're not always going to be able to do everything alone. You can be confident and competent and self-assured, and that is hugely important, but you should also know that it's not shameful to need others, to need a little help and support sometimes. There is nothing wrong with embracing human connection.

In the same way that you would be willing to provide support for a friend, know that you are not a burden for needing helping hands every now and again. Although you are doing this journey for you, you are a human, and humans need input and care from others sometimes.

Though it may feel difficult to imagine a time when your thoughts about yourself are entirely neutral, hold on to the hope that the day will come. It takes both time and hard work to make self-acceptance second nature, but it is possible to retrain your brain. Trust the process and stick at it, even when you feel that progress has plateaued, or you can't seem to shake certain thought patterns. Brains can be rigid, but they are also malleable – we can change the way we think, at any point, just like how, with intention, we can change our behaviours and learn new habits.

I hope you found this more practical section of the book helpful, and recognized the ways in which you may be holding yourself back from happiness, but also how you can change that and become kinder, and gentler, to yourself. Trusting yourself is incredibly freeing, and though it is totally natural to want a second opinion sometimes, you are much stronger and more capable than you realize. You have an instinctive, deep knowing of what is right for you – the more you connect with yourself, the more you will discover it, and the more confident you will be in taking charge of your life.

Though this journey may feel tiring at points, and you may struggle to visualize all of the progress you are making, these steps towards self-acceptance are some of the biggest and most rewarding you could take. A life spent hating yourself is no life at all, so even when the process feels long and tedious, keep pushing for a future where self-confidence comes naturally to you. You deserve it.

With that, it's important to recognize the hang-ups that many of us have which seem to justify our feeling of unworthiness. In the next part, we will dive deep into self-forgiveness, and how to untangle yourself from the ties of shame.

Understanding yourself and the root of your actions will pave the way for change.

Part 3
Forgive Yourself

In the original plan I made for this book, Part 3 didn't exist; I didn't think it necessary to include it. But as time went on, memories of the things I told myself when I was deep in self-hatred continued to rise to the surface. I remembered how I grappled, for a long time, with the feeling of not *deserving* good things. The act of forgiving myself has actually been a huge part of my journey.

While in the grips of a negative headspace, I told myself repeatedly that because I had hurt people in the past, I wasn't deserving of being kind to myself. I used every small but regrettable past action as ammunition. And the more I reminisced on these thoughts, the more I realized that actually, for some people, forgiving yourself may be the most substantial catalyst for change. It was a huge sticking point for me and something I've still been working on during the months I've been writing this book. Though it may not be relevant for everyone, I felt it necessary to include.

That's an important point to touch on in itself: your healing journey may not follow the order of this book. I am still, now, working on forgiving myself every day, and though I do not hold the anger I used to against the younger version of me and the mistakes I made during childhood, I feel it's important to acknowledge and be open about the fact that I am still making mistakes. I am still learning. I am, at the time of writing, 22 years old, and I do not have life all figured out. I still fumble and regret my actions, but with every mishap I learn to be kinder to myself and, as a by-product of that, to the world around me.

My old, polarized thinking patterns informed my reality, and it was a harsh and cruel rut in which many people will also have found themselves. Justifying your shame with every single small mistake you've made throughout your life comes hand in hand with the perfectionist mindset. As I have touched on, perfectionism for me was in many ways about control. I liked the definite things. I liked things to be one thing or another. Life, however, is not as binary as 'I deserve a bad life because I have not been 100 per cent morally perfect'. We all exist with good and bad inside of us, with the ability to behave in whichever way we choose. We won't always make the 'right' decisions, but that shouldn't condemn us to a miserable life.

In the following chapters I have opened up about a lot of stuff that I've not really told anyone before, because it is important to me that you know you are not alone and you are deserving of healing and forgiveness and kindness, whether or not in the past you have behaved in ways that you regret. I think it's easy to forget how human we all are, and to get swept up in the 'perfect person' ideal, especially as self-critical perfectionists.

Some things in this part may feel hard to confront, especially when touching on trauma-informed behaviours or life as an undiagnosed neurodivergent child, and so I want to remind you again that it is okay to dip in and out of the next few chapters. Come and go as you need, this book is here to help you. Use it at your own pace.

Chapter 9
Hurt People Hurt People

Self-hatred serves nobody.

The year was 2010 and the soft autumn sun hung low in the sky, filling the classroom with a familiar, warm light. This sort of sunlight, the kind that makes dust particles glisten as they float through the air, evokes nostalgia in me now. A nostalgia for a young, confused and nervously fidgety version of me, and for all of the feelings I associate with my time in primary school. Feelings that, though I have blocked out many memories from my school years, still make me squirm a little. I remember it so vividly. The memory of how it felt to be so uneasy, to feel so trapped, always waiting to be excluded from my current friendship group, to have it affirmed that I didn't belong, has never been lost on me.

I was a nine-year-old girl, full of feelings and a desperation to be accepted. I picked at the skin of my cuticles, further depleting my shredded nail beds as I tapped my foot against the floor. My chest ached in its state of perpetual tightness. I dreaded being here and I counted down the hours until I could leave. I had never had luck with making school friends, let alone keeping them. But, at this time, the friendship group I'd fallen in with seemed to like me. I did live in fear of ending up ostracized and alone again, but it was nice to be included for now. Though it didn't calm me down much, it was a relief to have a handle on one of my stressors.

One of the girls in my friendship group invited me to go to the toilet with her and I happily joined. I don't know why, as young girls, we tended to congregate in school toilets, but an invite to do so felt like a sign of inclusion in a friendship group.

It was a tight, eerie space, one in which I had heard too many ghost stories. There was only one small, rectangular window for light to come through. In the girls' toilets, untouched by the afternoon sun, the air was dingy and soulless. Paint peeled from the walls, messages were scribbled and carved into the wooden door. The air was dank and cold, as usual, but when Lily* asked if I wanted to go to the toilets with her, I counted my blessings. For little, nine-year-old me, it felt so good to finally have friends.

Lily and I stood side by side at the sinks, washing our hands. My eyes flitted between the running tap and the reflection of Lily in the mirror, hyper-aware I should make

---

* All names have been changed for privacy.

conversation. The water ran up to my wrists, dampening the sleeve of my fleece. I hated the feeling of wet sleeves, I still do. The silence made me hot and flustered. Something felt off. Two cubicle doors were open, one closed. It wasn't uncommon for one to be jammed shut because the school building was so old, so I told myself to brush off the anxiety I felt in my gut. As we dried our hands with scratchy blue paper towels, Lily turned to me, with a look on her face that I hadn't seen before. It unsettled me.

'Ro,' she asked. 'Don't you just hate Jess?' I observed her expression, relaxed and calm, though I was taken aback by her brashness. She met my eye. 'Isn't she so annoying?'

My palms grew clammy as a flicker of worry ran through me. I knew I shouldn't be unkind. I knew it was not nice to talk about people behind their backs. But it's also what all the cool girls did; you had to gossip to fit in. And it was so, so nice to have friends. I felt a great divide inside me. I glanced at the floor. Lily searched my face, waiting for my reply.

After some quiet deliberation and an awkwardly long pause, I responded. 'Ugh, yes,' I said, though I didn't mean it. I liked Jess; but equally, I wanted Lily to like me. I had to say the right thing, keep on their good sides, even if it felt wrong inside. And so, I agreed, trying to seem honest, *cool*. 'Yes, she's so annoying.'

As the words tumbled from my lips, the third cubicle door swung open. From the cubicle emerged the very girl I had just called annoying, Jess, with a glimmer in her eye and a look on her face about as scheming as a child could muster. 'I heard what you just said about me,' she spat.

I felt the walls close in on me, peeling paint and cobwebs smothering my small frame. *I was mean, I had said something unkind.* My throat closed up. *And she heard.* I couldn't breathe.

I ran from the girls' toilet, my face flooded with tears. They'd planned this. They'd planned to trip me up, to make me say something unkind, to see if I would say it.

In the moments after, I think I had my first ever anxiety attack. I remember curling up in a ball behind a blue standalone whiteboard and sobbing into my fists until my eyes were bloodshot. I remember wanting to crawl out of my skin. I remember that when the teacher asked what was wrong, I couldn't reply because I felt it was my fault for being unkind. I remember thinking I was rotten to the core – a truly horrible person.

And in that moment, my world came crumbling down. It was nice to have friends, but I was sure I'd lost them now. I knew they'd sat and planned this together, and I knew that meant they didn't really like me.

I wouldn't have said it if I'd have known she'd have heard, but that didn't reassure my conscience. I shouldn't have said something unkind, and I knew that was where I'd gone wrong. You shouldn't say something about someone if you're not prepared for them to hear it. I'd been taught that years ago. The bit that hurt the most, though, was that no part of me even believed what I'd said. Those words were backed only by my utter desperation to be liked, to be accepted, to not be alone. I didn't know how to speak up for myself, nor to voice my own opinions. I got through life as a social chameleon, changing to fit in with whoever would have me. It was beside the point, though; nothing changed the fact that I'd chosen to be unkind.

This wasn't the first time in my childhood I'd spoken about others behind their back; regretfully I had found myself joining in with gossiping time and time again. The only difference was that the person being spoken about had never overheard, so I'd never had this part of myself I so disliked being exposed. I felt a lot of guilt every time I engaged in unkind conversations.

I don't want to paint a false picture, however. I have by no means been faultless in adulthood. Deep down, I knew, and still know, the normalized gossiping I engaged in clashed with my morals and wasn't indicative of the person I wanted to be. But humans make mistakes, and they will continue to make mistakes. You will have said and done things that you regret. You may have held onto grudges you wish you'd let go of sooner, behaved in ways that were inauthentic to you, or let fear stop you from growing and changing. You will have made mistakes. So have I, in adulthood as well as childhood. As has everyone.

According to a study by researchers from the Universities of Maryland and Stanford, which used a computer simulation to mimic human behaviour, researchers investigated whether people would engage in gossip that was happening, be it to benefit themselves or to harm others. By the end of the simulation, 90 per cent of the simulated agents had chosen to engage in gossip.* Gossiping, though it can leave you feeling unkind, is an incredibly normal part of socialization. We should strive to treat others with kindness, but we must understand that, as humans, we aren't infallible. Chastizing ourselves with guilt isn't constructive.

We will not always walk through this world as our kindest, best self. You are not always going to handle things in the way you want to. That is the nature of being human. There is a pressure to be wise and have a handle on everything we feel, and that would be wonderful, but give yourself some grace. This is your first time living!

You can be a wonderful person and still do unkind things. You can have made mistakes and done things that have hurt others, yet you still deserve happiness, still deserve a good life. Acknowledging that you want to be kind matters most.

Hurting and hurting

As a child, the unkind things I'd said would keep me up at night, anxious thoughts swirling around in my mind. *Why*

---

* Pan, Xinyue, et al., 'Explaining the evolution of gossip', Proceedings of the National Academy of Sciences of the United States of America, February 20, 2024 (www.pnas.org/doi/10.1073/pnas.2214160121)

did I say that? Why was I so horrible? Staring at my ceiling, I lay awake, berating myself, replaying the experience over and over.

I didn't have the answers then, but I do now. And it is not an excuse, but a reason.

I did it because I was hurting.

My therapist spoke with me recently about how everything we feel and do has at some point intended to help us. We do things out of a need to survive, as an act of self-protection. This has always made a lot of sense to me in the context of anxiety and fear, but I hadn't ever considered that my behaviour as a child was a survival tactic. As I think about it, I can feel my throat getting tight, and I find myself filled with emotions – of grief and forgiveness and acceptance. It's hard not to ache for the version of me that I spent so long chastizing for coping in the only way she knew how to.

I did it because that was how I'd learned to survive the social situations I struggled in. I did it because I thought it was what people did to make friends. Hurt people hurt people. I was hurt, I was actively hurting, in fact. I was trying to make it through school alive. I was trying to keep my head above water. And I was able to hurt others because I thought it would help me, that it would make people like me. I just wanted to be like the other girls.

Truthfully, I've been squirming writing this chapter. Though I don't blame my younger self at all anymore and I understand my behaviour at that time, I went against my own morals. I wasn't proud of it then and it still feels uncomfortable to admit now.

I felt rotten, horrid at my core, for years. I didn't have the information that I have now and I didn't understand that I was allowed to forgive myself when I did something regrettable. That humans can do unkind things and still have good inside of them. I felt the only reasonable explanation was that I was a bad person. But I see now, so clearly, that I wasn't a 'bad' person at all. I was a person in pain.

There are many reasons why we humans lash out when we are hurting. Sometimes it may be that we were hurt before, that we haven't processed the emotions we feel around that situation, and so they come out in aggressive or unkind ways. It can also, in some cases, be a projection of insecurity and pain onto others. And, as was the way in my life, when we succumb to people-pleasing tendencies, we can do things we disagree with deep down and we can hurt people. We can betray our own morals, do things that do not feel true to us, things we later regret. This is not to say it's okay to hurt people because you are hurting, but just that it's okay to forgive yourself for doing so.

Before we can begin the journey to the healed version of ourselves (which, admittedly, is in some ways a lifelong journey), we must acknowledge the hurt version of us and forgive them.

Breaking the cycle

Sometimes I like to imagine myself as a Russian doll. If you were to open me up you'd find another, smaller version of me, and that version of me holds another, smaller past version of me. Inside me are all of my past selves. I still carry with me all the people I have been, and they carry all of the things that have hurt me, changed me, helped me and made me who I am today.

It is well known that there is a cyclical nature of emotional pain. Those who have been hurt in their life are often prone to hurting others. We are not all-knowing beings. We cannot control the effect that trauma and emotional pain has on us. Sometimes it takes having hurt people to even realize that trauma is responsible for our behaviour.

Instead of beating yourself up for your past actions, try to hold that version of you with empathy and forgiveness. You may have hurt other people in the past, but the fact that you have regret for that is what is important. The past version of you didn't know any better, you acted in a way that felt right at the time, and that's what you needed in order to get through that period. We sometimes have to live through experiences we come to regret in order to find the person we want to be. We can use our mistakes to learn about ourselves and why we behave the way we do. Once you have been hurt, the healing process can be hard to find your way to and you may end up trying on a lot of masks to hide the struggle within. Do not let shame weigh you down; you are allowed to leave the way you acted when you were hurting in the past. It is incredibly brave to even try to heal. The realization that you want to be different, that you don't want to pass on your pain, is where you hold your power.

If hurt people hurt people, then being kinder to yourself now will make you kinder to others.

I have long been riddled with imposter syndrome. It's a way my anxiety manifests, ruminating on the parts of me that are less than 'perfect' and believing that they make me fraudulent. If people like me, or love me, my anxiety tries to convince me that it's because they haven't yet seen the *real* me. They love the version of me that I show the world. And yes, to a degree, we are all masking in some form. We all show the world the best version of ourselves. But as it does most things, my anxious brain blows things out of proportion and equates being a human who makes mistakes with being the worst person in the world. Imposter syndrome tells me that I'm simply playing a good person, fooling those around me by hiding my true self, that at my core I am *bad*.

If I could talk to that younger version of me, I would tell her to cut herself some slack. You aren't a horrible, awful person. For a good chunk of my life, I lived with a deep guilt and an inexplicable fear that everyone was going to eventually find out I was a terrible person. My entire being was shrouded in shame, effectively because I couldn't give myself grace for the fact that I used to lash out when I felt threatened. I was a product of my pain, and I did things I regretted because of it, but the fact that I recognized immediately that it was unkind and wrong to say things about others, the fact that it clashed so much with what I believed, was evidence enough that I was not actually a person with no morals. I was just doing my best with what I had at the time, and unfortunately that meant I picked up some coping mechanisms I wasn't fond of.

This is potentially a niche anxiety that you may not relate to, but I want to write this for the people who will find themselves reflected in these words; the people who understand exactly how it feels to be so convinced you're secretly terrible. There is not going to come a day when people find out about the real you. *This is the real you.* Your small flaws and human slip-ups do not erase the good parts of you. You, like every other human, have good and bad in you, and in your past. People will love you for you, and if at the same time you make mistakes and do things you regret? You will still be the person they love. And the people who you worry are going to see the 'real you' one day are not infallible either.

You are *not* rotten to your core. You are anxious. The fear that everybody is going to one day find out who you 'truly' are and dislike you for it is your perfectionism trying to vilify standard parts of the human experience. It's also anxiety convincing you that your past actions define your entire personality.

As I write this, there are still thinking patterns I have that I do not like. There is a part of me that I am slowly untangling myself from, a bit of me who learned in childhood to put my guard up and not trust others, to assume the worst in people. This has, at times, led me to judge people unfairly. I'm not proud of that but I know that the parts of myself that do not reflect my moral conscience are products of my experiences, they are not fundamentally who I am.

This chapter may also have made you confront things you'd rather not think about. That is totally natural. We all avoid thinking about events that bring up feelings of shame. Letting go of shame around our past actions is a huge part of healing our relationship with ourselves. We cannot move on and live freely if we are still tortured about things we regret.

Though it's a hard pill to swallow, you cannot change your past. You cannot undo any hurt you may have accidentally, or perhaps intentionally at the time, caused. Living with shame will hold you back. It's okay to forgive yourself. You don't always need to be holding yourself accountable. You're not a self-improvement project, you're a human, and you are allowed to get it wrong sometimes.

When trying to achieve a feeling of neutrality and forgiveness for our past selves, it may be helpful to confront the memories of times when you acted in a way that you later came to regret.

Forgiving your past self

Can you remember a time when you know you hurt somebody?

It may feel uncomfortable to think about, but a reminder: you can be a good person and do 'bad' things. If you can remember, take a moment to reflect on what was going on for you at that time. For example, when I remember joining in on being unkind about others, I had not long experienced being excluded from a friendship group and had been bullied.

Were there any experiences that may have impacted your behaviour? Perhaps, if there were, this can help you understand your actions and have some forgiveness for your past self. You behaved in a way that served you at the time.

We should all try to treat others with the same kindness and respect we would want to be shown. However, if you do slip up and you don't act in a way that's reflective of that, the key to moving forward isn't to double down, it's to make peace with your actions. Being angry at yourself will make you push frustration onto the outside world and inadvertently cause further hurt and the cycle will continue. Understanding yourself and the root of your actions will pave the way for change.

The first step is always to forgive yourself. All human behaviour has an explanation. It is important to apologize to those you have hurt. But you also owe an apology to yourself, for being unkind to yourself, and for being so angry at yourself while you were figuring out how to cope with pain. Self-hatred serves nobody, and as the next chapter says – humans make mistakes.

Chapter 10
Humans Make Mistakes

There is no such thing as a good or bad person. There are only people.

While I don't mean to say it's okay to hurt others, I do think it's important to face the fact that, as is the nature of being human, you are going to continue to make mistakes. Every season of life will present its challenges, and with them may come reactions, events and displays of behaviour that you won't feel proud of. You are never going to be perfect, and you need to stop holding yourself to a standard that nobody (and I mean nobody) will ever meet.

I can think of multiple times in recent years when I have said or done something I have come to regret. I have argued with the people I love most. I have said things I don't mean.

I can also think of multiple things I have done for the good of others. I have made people I love happy by actions that were thoughtful, kind and caring.

When asked to describe myself, I would never say 'argumentative' or 'unkind'. However, I *would* describe myself as 'kind', 'caring' and 'thoughtful'. It is not my actions that define me, but the intention behind them, and the way they made me feel. If I were to live my life judging myself on behaviours that I exhibited when I was in my most vulnerable, heightened state, when I had no time to think through what I was saying or doing, and felt immediate regret, I would never allow myself to feel joy.

The people who are described as 'not having a bad bone in their body'? They make mistakes sometimes! Because, contrary to popular belief, there is no such thing as bad bones. There is no such thing as a good or bad person. There are only people, with good and bad inside of them, and everyone is born with the capability to behave in ways that help or harm others.

Sometimes you will be unkind. Sometimes you will snap back and say hurtful things and regret them once the heat of the moment has passed. Sometimes you'll wonder how you can think such unkind thoughts. You're not supposed to have it all figured out. We all have parts of ourselves that come out when our filter slips, when emotions trigger us into a reactive state. We all have that primal, fighting part of our persona. That doesn't mean you should write yourself off, or deny yourself happiness. You aren't a bad person, you're a human.

Accepting that I am always going to make mistakes has helped me stop being overly critical of myself when I do. If I had arguments with people I loved, I used to struggle to see that it was a totally normal part of growing up and family life, and that when saying something I regretted, what mattered most was that I did regret it (and that I apologized). Accepting that I wasn't always going to be the 'best' version of me but all I could do was try to lead with a kind heart and good intention, brought me an ability to be more gentle with myself than I ever had before.

When I think about what it takes to forgive another person, it is imperative to try to understand their perspective. Understanding the emotions they were experiencing and their thought processes can help us to give others a little more grace, and to acknowledge that they made a mistake because they too are human and they may be dealing with something. But we never seem to extend this to ourselves. We rarely allow ourselves to pick apart the origins of our behaviour, to understand why we react in the ways we do. The root of our behaviour is the key to changing it and to forgiving ourselves.

It brings me back to the point that I have made over and over again while writing this book. One of the best things you can do for yourself during your healing journey is to let go of the expectations you put upon yourself to be perfect. In fact, let go of your concept of perfect altogether.

All you can do when mistakes are made is be honest. Honesty with yourself, and others, is the best way to resolve hurt. Acknowledging what you've done wrong, being able to confront aspects of yourself that may cause struggles in your relationships, to hold up the tender, unhealed parts of you to the light and say, 'I am sorry for how I hurt you, this human part of me needs some attention and affection and I will work on healing it'. Building authenticity in your relationships and being open about the fact there are things to work on, is a beautiful thing. Not only will it help others approach you and have open communication about things that may be hurting them without you knowing, but it also takes the pressure off you a little. You are not putting out a version of you that you are determined for everyone to know and believe that you are perfect, infallible, the ultimate version of yourself. You're able to say, 'I'm messy sometimes, and if it ever upsets you, let's talk about it and I will continue to work on myself'.

You are not damaged beyond repair, or horrible, or unloveable. You are navigating life and love and learning about yourself through those. And that, naturally, can be very overwhelming.

Making peace

Imagine if somebody had hurt you. Maybe they said something unkind or behaved in a way that upset you. It's natural to feel a mix of anger and confusion. You might wish they would recognize the impact of their actions so you can process your feelings and move forward.

Now, picture them apologizing to you. Picture a genuine, heartfelt apology. Visualize the person who hurt you recognizing your feelings and that their behaviour has caused you pain. It's not 'I'm sorry you feel this way', but 'I'm sorry I behaved in that way'. There are some things that can't be fixed with an apology, but providing what the person had done wasn't a huge red flag, for me, a genuine apology and asking for forgiveness allows me to let go of the anger I'm feeling.

With that being said, I do know it is not easy to *just forgive everyone*. There are situations where forgiveness isn't an easy concept to grapple with. Anger serves a purpose, and I know all too well the injustice of being hurt by somebody who will never acknowledge their wrongdoing.

But forgiveness is not the same as reconciliation. Forgiveness is for your own good.

And in my experience, my self-blame was intertwined with the anger I felt towards those who had hurt me. It was confronting both, which ultimately allowed me to begin healing and move on.

Though it is so hard to forgive people who have caused such hurt and pain in your life, holding onto anger at someone who will never apologize will hurt you more than it'll ever hurt them. It'll eat away at your life. I found myself such an angry person, so untrusting of the world. I turned much of that unresolved anger in on myself, because as a lot of people with trauma will know, it's very easy to blame yourself for things that weren't your fault. It made me miserable.

And, as somebody who has experienced trauma, I found my anger left me quite resistant to forgiveness. I was tied up in emotion, being unduly hard on myself. Any conversations that could bring me closure will likely never happen. That is an unfortunate fact that I have had to face up to. There are people in this world who will never see their wrongs. It hurts. But I will not let it stop me from leading with kindness and forgiveness in my own life.

Making peace with your past doesn't mean they've 'won' or that what happened to you doesn't matter. It took me a long time to realize that holding a grudge and living inside anger didn't have an impact on the person I was hurt by whatsoever, it only made me miserable. All that resentment did was sabotage and hurt me.

So, I started by forgiving myself.

A letter of forgiveness

When you get a moment alone and are in a headspace to face the event(s) for which you hold guilt, I'd like you to write a letter to yourself. You can either address this 'Dear me' or 'Dear past me', whichever feels right to you. Writing on physical paper is preferable, but if that isn't available to you then a Word document or your Notes app will work too. One important thing to remember before you begin: nobody but you is going to read this letter. The most freeing part about this is that once you have finished, you are going to dispose of what you've written. So, make sure you get everything that comes to mind onto the page – this piece of paper is a non-judgemental, safe space, just for you.

Bring to mind the event(s) that you feel blame or guilt around. How do they make you feel about yourself? How has your guilt impacted you since? Let it all flow out. Each part of this can be led by you, and can be as long or as short as you like.

If you are struggling to get started, here is an example:

Dear past me,

I have always been so angry at you for what you did. I wish it was handled better and I hate that it happened...

The guilt I have felt for so many years has made me feel worthless, and as though I am not deserving of good things.

Now, think about how you wish you'd have behaved or dealt with the situation. What have you learned since? Have you taken any steps to move away from certain behaviours?

Example:

If I had my time again, I wouldn't have said what I did, and I'd have thought before I acted. The person I am now is growing and learning, and one of the things I now do before I act on my anger/hurt is this...

Now that you've got all of your anger or resentment onto the page, it's time for self-compassion. You are human. You do not deserve to spend the rest of your life beating yourself up about the past. You cannot control what has been and gone, you can only create a brighter future.

Example:

Although I have held onto this anger for a long time, I want you to know that I am letting it go. I forgive you, now. I know that it's okay that you made mistakes. Mistakes don't define me anymore, and I will show myself compassion. I deserve love and I deserve good things, and you did too, you were just hurting/young/learning.

Make a commitment to yourself now and to future you. What are you going to change so that you don't have to live with guilt and regret over any future mistakes?
Example:

I know now that I am not a bad person if I make mistakes. I am trying to live as kindly as possible, but I am human and I may struggle sometimes. I will try my hardest not to beat myself up or self-sabotage if I do something I regret in the future...

From, Me

Putting pen to paper and expressing resentment or difficult feelings towards your past takes immense strength. Take a deep breath and know that you should feel so proud. If you like, you can read your letter back as many times as you need to, or until you feel what you've written has sunk in.

The final step of this exercise is to dispose of the letter. Tear it up, burn it, paint over it, delete it. You've written that you're going to let your anger go, and this is the physical representation of that. Do this in whichever way works for you, but stay safe – please only set fire to the letter if you have proper fire safety precautions in place.

For me, trying to leave the past in the past means forgiving life for dealing me the cards it did. Forgiving the universe for the fact that you won't get an apology sometimes. Forgiving yourself, wholly, for how you have reacted to painful situations. You have always done your best with what you knew at the time. And you are allowed to feel anger at those who hurt you, as well as anger at your past actions, but do not let that anger dictate your life or impact your treatment of others. You are worth more than a life stuck in that cycle.

Forgiving myself was an act of self-compassion and self-acceptance. It was the moment when I stopped worrying that I was a terrible person. I hadn't realized how much of a block to true happiness that worry had been.

You deserve to forgive yourself. You deserve to let go of the past. You deserve to move on from things you have grown beyond. You cannot grow if you continue to bully yourself over things that weren't your fault or actions that don't represent the true you.

You are allowed to start again, every day. You can end up living in a cycle of being triggered and re-triggering yourself if you hyperfixate on your every thought, every word, if you are endlessly trying to dissect others' true intentions. Society teaches us that the best thing to be is kind. But to me, the best thing to be is perfectly imperfect. To admit when you have been wrong. To take any mishaps in your stride. To always do your best to be your most understanding, nurturing and forgiving self but to understand, nurture and forgive yourself when you can't be.

'The world is cruel, therefore I won't be.'

I have kept this quote close to my heart throughout my healing journey. Despite what has happened to me in life, I won't let it make me cruel. I won't be unkind to others, and I won't be unkind to myself. But if I slip up, if I, or somebody else, is spiteful towards me – I know now how to forgive.

There is good in this world, and I know that because there are so many people who, like me, try to turn their pain into helping others. Yes, humans have made mistakes that have hurt me. Humans can be incredibly vindictive. But humans can also be selfless and kind and I will not let their occasional cruelty stop me from nurturing a loving relationship with myself. I will not let their cruelty stop me from seeing the light in the world, from feeling the sun upon my skin, from opening my heart to people who only want to cherish it and nurture it.

It will not serve you to constantly live in the memory of every mistake you've ever made. You have the power to choose to be kind to yourself and others in any situation, in any relationship, going forward. That is what you need to focus on, that is what matters.

Time plays a crucial role in forgiveness. Take the time pressure off yourself, don't be in such a rush. It may take a while to forgive yourself and others. After all, we hold grudges because the event or situation really hurt us. Healing takes time.

It won't always feel like the best thing in the moment, in fact, it might feel like a part of you is breaking; I know that though forgiveness seems honourable it can really be quite painful to let go. The truth is that parts of this journey will challenge you, and won't always sit 'right' with you, because this new way of being kinder and gentler with yourself isn't your norm.

You're going to have days when things feel really difficult and you wonder if you're doing this whole healing thing 'correctly'. You are. And I know that if you're a person who likes order and routine, being told that things won't always go to plan can feel intimidating. But if you avoid putting the work into healing through fear of the unknown, you will be stuck in the same behaviours forever.

During my eating disorder recovery, I constantly had to remind myself: the struggle of a day in recovery will never be as bad as the struggle of a day spent unwell. The same applies to any healing journey. Though it may feel safer to do things in the way you're used to, you will never find joy by choosing a familiar pain over unfamiliar healing. And if you always do what you've always done, you'll always get what you've always got. As long as you are moving forward, as long as you are trying to be kinder to yourself, you are healing. You are doing it 'right'.

Chapter 11
You Deserve Good Things

You are trying, and that is all that matters.

My childhood home was comfortably quiet, silence briefly interrupted only by a pitter-patter of little paws, or the sound of Mum making dinner in the kitchen below me. The sunset cast a gentle glow upon my room, orange and warm and reminiscent of a hug. My favourite little trinkets sat on my bookshelf; tiny ceramic houses, a collection of stones from various beaches, little ornaments cherry-picked by friends on trips abroad. They're arranged just the way I liked them: the houses in a neat row, and the rest a muddled constellation. They reflected the golden light, each of them small glimmers of joy, of moments I felt happiest. I was not in a happy place but they reminded me that I will be again, because I have been before.

Today, I survived. Today, I ate. Today, I stepped out of my room and walked to the bathroom and I brushed my teeth. The task of washing my face felt insurmountable the day before, but today I had twisted the tap and cupped my palms beneath the flowing water, and as I felt the cold splash against my skin, I was proud of myself.

Today was a good day.

Did I start a business or run a marathon?

No, no I didn't.

I had what, to some, would be an unfathomably unproductive day. But to me, it was a success. I sat with myself and I said: *it's okay. I will do what I can. I am me, and I don't have to be like the people I compare myself to. I cannot do all that they can, because I am me, and they are them. It is still a good day because I know that when the walls feel as though they are closing in and life is a lead weight sitting upon your chest, the walk to the bathroom is a marathon.*

My good days will not look like others' good days because my brain doesn't work the same way. I no longer tell myself that I am making excuses, or that I am simply lazy. I give myself one task and one task only – try to survive. When that feels easier, I try to be 1 per cent kinder to myself every day. And better is fluid, better isn't cumulative. I may find myself unable to get out of bed on Tuesday but on Wednesday, I will try again. I am still moving towards healing, still moving in the right direction. I am doing just fine. The things that others find easy just take me a little longer. I have made peace with that.

One per cent is all it takes

In the times when I find myself infuriated with my inability to be productive, I remind myself of this: I didn't choose to struggle with basic tasks. I didn't choose to struggle with motivation. I didn't choose to be exhausted after a day of socializing. I didn't choose to have this brain. The blame does not fall on me, the blame belongs to society, for the fact that for so long I believed I was only deserving of happiness and joy and the beauty the world has to offer if I was ultra-productive. If I made no mistakes. If I was picture perfect. If I fulfilled every new expectation the world put upon me, even if it meant I started crumbling.

For so long – too long – I blocked out the light the world offered me because I felt undeserving. I have been offered incredible opportunities, and though I have taken some of them, I have done so while convincing myself that I am a fraud, an imposter, utterly undeserving of basking in any of my own glory. The brain I was given isn't attuned to appreciate small joys, instead telling me I do not deserve them.

What makes me sad is that I know there are so, so many people just like me. The version of me who used to sleep for eighteen hours a day, who couldn't face life, who didn't want to move from my bed to the sofa, or eat, or drink, or brush my teeth. She still exists. I don't exhibit these behaviours anymore, but there is an abundance of beautiful people out there in the world who mirror the girl I was and who have also fallen into the toxic productivity hellscape. Who struggle to do enough to feel proud because it doesn't feel like enough for this world.

Will it ever be enough? There will always be an influencer with a 5–9 before their 9–5, who wakes up earlier than you and has no issue rising from their slumber, who is bouncy and excited for the day, who can fit in a run and a cooked breakfast and a meditative journaling session all before 7 a.m. For people like me, to manage just one of those things would make my week. But people like me do not often allow ourselves to feel the joy of little wins. We only ever see what we are not managing, what we have not completed. We are forever fighting against ourselves. It is rarely, *well done me, I found showering hard today and I still did it.* It's: *oh great, I finally showered, and now it's done, but it shouldn't have taken that much effort. And all I can focus on is my never-ending to-do list that I seem incapable of mastering. I bet anyone else could fit all of this into an hour.*

It's time to stop focusing on what 'they' are doing. You are not them and they are not you, and that is a wonderful thing! You have your own struggles, perhaps, but that doesn't make you lesser, or weak. Forgive yourself for the things you cannot control, and shift the focus to all that you do manage to do, rather than scolding yourself for what you don't. You also have your own capabilities and I know for sure there are things that you will be good at that others aren't. It's time you let yourself celebrate your achievements.

Small wins are still wins. You deserve to celebrate things that are important to *you*. The small joys in life are found when we acknowledge the things that feel important to us, not what is impressive to others.

The Grateful Heart, a study by McCraty & Childre (2004), showed that people who practised gratitude had lower levels of cortisol (the stress hormone) than those who didn't. Taking a little time out of your day to make note of the good in your life can help to regulate, and reduce, feelings of anxiety and depression.*

As I have learned through my own experience, when you begin to let light in, it opens the door to a new way of viewing the world. It's never as simple as just 'looking on the bright side', but when you can find happiness in trivial, everyday things, you will begin to see beauty everywhere, in everything. To actively acknowledge your personal wins, to allow yourself to feel the sun on your skin, to believe you are deserving of the love you give others, is a joy that I hope you all will get to experience. You deserve to.

---

* McCraty, R., and Childre, D., 'The Grateful Heart: The Psychophysiology of Appreciation', 2004 (https://psycnet.apa.org/record/2004-00298-012)

No win is too small

What if you allowed yourself to acknowledge your achievements within their relativity to your life?

Grab a paper and pen, or open the Notes app on your phone. Answer this one thing: what would you feel proud of yourself for today if the world celebrated the small wins in the way we do the big wins?

No achievement is silly or irrelevant. If you have accomplished something you doubted you could, you have a reason to be proud of yourself.

You deserve good things. Whether your biggest achievement this week has been getting out of bed, or brushing your teeth, or picking up this book, you deserve good things. If you have rested and missed deadlines and procrastinated important tasks. You still deserve good things. If you have hurt somebody or said something you regret or snapped without meaning to. You. Still. Deserve. Good. Things.

In Chapter 6 we discussed letting go of perfection during this healing journey, but I also need you to know that it is okay to let go of perfection in all areas of your life. You're never going to do everything right. You're never going to be the best at everything. You're not always going to be as kind to everyone as you would like. You are only human. You don't owe this world perfection. All you can do is try to walk through life as the person you want to be, but you are going to slip up sometimes and still you will be worthy of good things.

It is very freeing to realize that you are not ever going to be perfect. And it is euphoric when you finally feel okay in that. You are going to be messy and struggle and cry and argue and get things wrong. And so what?! You are trying, and that is all that matters. You will make mistakes. You will forgive yourself. And the world will keep on spinning.

Sitting cross-legged on my bed, held by the orange glow of my bedroom, I picked up my pen and reached for my journal. I wrote down what I was proud of myself for, just like I did every day. *Today I am proud that I looked after myself.* I was proud that I showed myself kindness. I have a brain that works against me and I have had many days where I couldn't take care of myself. This is something to be celebrated. To me, this is a huge win. I allowed myself to feel this pride because I know that although I haven't had a productive day by everyone's standards, I gave it my all, and that is enough.

What are you proud of yourself for today?

This part of the book may have brought up uncomfortable feelings. To look our past in the face, to sit in the discomfort of acknowledging that we have been unkind or hurt people, and to then forgive ourselves for it, is incredibly brave.

Letting light and love into our lives also means allowing yourself to feel it and know in your heart that you are worthy of it. That despite the guilt we carry, or past actions we regret, we are not 'bad' people.

I hope you know that your mistakes are not flaws but opportunities for personal growth. I hope you know that you will be your best, and happiest, self when you believe that you deserve to be.

People who acknowledge their wrongdoings and face them head on are those who I trust the most in this world. Living riddled with guilt and shame will not make you a happier or better human, but forgiving yourself and giving yourself permission to move on and show yourself kindness will. That is true growth.

Bad and good, kindness and cruelty, joy and anger, exist within every single human on Earth. Without one, we wouldn't know the other. There is no joy without pain. It's this duality, this complexity, that defines the human experience. In the pursuit of knowing and accepting ourselves wholly, we must embrace it all.

You are the one person who can always be in your corner.

Part 4
Be Kind to Yourself

In these final chapters, we will focus on the importance of maintaining the changes you have worked so hard to implement. As I have shared, my healing journey wasn't a linear one, and life is turbulent. There may be times where you notice you are slipping back into old ways, but that is not a sign of weakness or failure, it's a chance to revisit and strengthen what you've learned. Those moments are when you must fight the hardest. No matter what, keep being kind to yourself. This part is here to demystify the meaning of health, share top tips to maintain your positive self-talk, help you set boundaries and eliminate people-pleasing and, finally, understand who you really are.

Chapter 12
Fundamental Health

Health looks different on everybody.

Before I've even propped myself up in bed in the morning, I will have consumed social media content about other people's lives. One of the first things I do after I wake – unfortunately a tendency that has become somewhat addictive – is to scroll. And, as I go about my day, I will continue to be delivered masses of information from thousands of individuals, a wealth of confident contradictions from one video to the next. All of them delivered with assertion, telling me precisely how I should, and shouldn't, be living. I know that being bombarded with health-focused content only fuels the anxiety that made me sick in the first place, and so, reflexively, I press the button to let the algorithm know I'm not interested.

I have been told time and time again: 'you control your algorithm'. And I know that. The algorithm of social media sites tailors the content I see to what I have shown an interest in. But many people can't understand just how hard it is to effectively make the statement: 'I am not interested in seeing content about weight loss and healthy eating'.

You may find yourself reflected in these words and have not, until now, realized that the tightness that rises in your chest as you scroll is actually anxiety. Or you may know you are quite sensitive to dialogue around health and fitness and make every effort to avoid it. Whichever you feel resonates, I hope this chapter will serve to remind you that true happiness does not stem from so-called 'clean' eating, weight loss or excessive exercising. Health is not one size fits all.

I want this book to be a safe space for you, and I wanted to include this chapter on 'health' to help silence the constant noise and looming pressure of an ever-growing fitness industry. For some people, the effects of growing up in a fatphobic, diet-culture-riddled society can be devastating when it comes to self-image. Others, meanwhile, may not be affected to the same degree. But there is a reason this chapter is placed so late on in this book and that is because although I feel the health and fitness world's toxicity is necessary to address, it is unlikely to change. And even if it did, that wouldn't bring immediate healing.

I think the most important thing is for you to be able to empower yourself. I want you to see yourself as deserving of kindness for reasons that exist within you, not just based on challenging your perception of health. You are so much more than 'health' or weight, what you eat or how you exercise. One of the biggest triggers for my own negative self-talk was the pressure I placed upon myself to be 'healthy'. Healing happens from the inside out, and my aspiration is that throughout this book you have been able to recognize the limitless wonders of *you*, and that now, in this final part, you can learn to protect yourself from outside influences. This world, and society, will continue to present new and unforeseen challenges as technology and humanity develop. As individuals, we cannot prevent that. However, we *can* shield our positive self-talk from being infiltrated by what may arise in the future.

I hope that as you continue through this journey and cultivate and expand on the knowledge you have taken from this book, you will come to find a safe space within yourself.

Let's check in: how are you feeling? Here is your reminder to do something kind for yourself today. Continue to check in on yourself throughout this part, and regularly once you have finished this book. Stay connected with yourself. You already have everything you need to protect yourself within you, and this part is about nurturing that.

What does healthy even mean?

It's not just because of personal difficulties with my body and food that I have struggled to reject health and fitness content. Like many others, I grew up in a society that led me to believe I should always put my physical appearance first. No matter what size you are, *you should* be losing weight, 'toning up' and engaging in some form of a diet. It feels like cultural sacrilege to refuse to do so.

Inundated by content centred around health, fitness, calories and demonizing foods, it's not easy to say, 'I actually don't want to know'. For that reason, it was such a struggle for me to begin to detoxify my for-you page, or any similarly personalized feed of content. There was a part of me that knew what was best for my mental health and that content of that vein made me feel terrible, but, as was the nature of my illness, there would always be a little part of my brain that came alive when I was presented with a weight loss tip, or a 'healthy swap' infographic. It was a persistent poke at a part of me trying fiercely to heal. I did the hard thing each and every time those posts came up for me and eventually the algorithm listened and learned.

Though I have now, for the most part, trained my algorithm not to recommend unhelpful content, I'm sure others will struggle to make that step. I need you to remember this: saying you are not interested in obsessive health and fitness content is not saying you don't care about your health. It is, in fact, the total opposite.

In the media and on social media, health is largely focused on weight and body types; two things that cannot be used as an accurate measure. This appearance-centric approach totally overlooks the bigger picture; the many components (mental happiness, social relationships, job satisfaction, enjoying movement, finding your purpose) that make up a true 'healthy lifestyle'. You are allowed to reject this outdated idea of 'health'. You are allowed to think, and do, differently.

What are the fundamentals of health? It's a topic that has been both over-simplified and over-complicated, measured by little more than a person's figure, with new trends, rules and recommendations surfacing all the time.

Do you really have to do 20k steps daily, be training for a marathon, have lettuce instead of bread and swap all your favourite foods for 'lighter' options to be healthy? Does a miserably rigid routine which makes you dread the day ahead equate to good health? Defining wellness in such a prescriptive way can end up doing one of two things: alienating those who don't want to live this way from 'wellness' altogether, or making those who believe they have to do these things to be healthy, miserable.

Some people absolutely will feel their healthiest when they are engaging in traditional 'wellness' practices, some will have a middle ground and some will be like me – people for whom it is healthier to run far, far away from those behaviours than it is to engage in any of them. For people with a history like mine, those behaviours will quickly become impulsive and obsessive and will suck the life out of you. I feel my healthiest when I do none of the things listed above. Wellness, to me, looks like exercising in a fun way (such as climbing or racquet sports) every so often and eating my five-a-day, but also allowing myself a sweet treat (or two, or three) every day.

When the picture of health is marketed as one size fits all, the unique needs and abilities of individuals are ignored, and anyone who cannot meet the current standards is excluded. Despite often hearing that 'it's all about balance', there is little scope for balance in society's current health trend cycles. Even the language used around health and fitness is riddled with shame – 'guilt-free foods', 'cheat day', 'detoxing', 'going on a cleanse', 'I've been so *bad*' – the list goes on. Is it any wonder we find it so hard not to be binary in our views of 'health'?

True wellness is about redressing the balance between pushing yourself and protecting yourself. It's finding what works for you while holding on to the knowledge that you can have a totally individual approach to fitness and still be healthy and worthwhile. Your body, your life, your passions, your hobbies – none of them will be exactly the same as anybody else's. Your version of a healthy life won't either. Some days you may feel energetic and excited about moving your body, while on others you may want nothing more than to snuggle under a blanket in front of the TV with a comfort film. That is okay!

Do not listen to anyone who tells you that you lack discipline because you don't want to engage in fitness the way they do. You do not need to feel guilt for the fact that your body requires rest. The key to health is to listen to both your body and your mind and choose what is going to make you happiest in that moment, regardless of what anybody else is doing.

At an age where I was most impressionable, I was sold a lie. I followed the YouTube workouts which promised me toned legs, slim arms and an hourglass figure, like a religion. I chased the ultimate 'healthy lifestyle' and the result was that I ended up in my most unhealthy, unhappy state. When my world centred around society's definition of 'healthy', I was miserable.

Not only was I depressed as I floated through life in a haze, my mind consumed with obsessive thoughts about weight and workouts, but I was also physically suffering. Underfuelled and overworked, as I'd stand up from my exercise mat after I'd followed another routine promising me the firm arms I lusted after, the room would spin. I'd have to steady myself on whatever was closest to me. I assumed this was just the price people paid for a 'perfect' body. With each shower, I would see my hair thin more and more, the plughole clogged with clumps of it. My rosy glow faded as my cheeks sunk into my face, a deathly pale wash appearing in its place. The body I was told I was building up, I was actually running into the ground.

It is rarely spoken of, the risks of taking exercise and dieting too far; you are never given the warnings you need to hear... Warning: the pursuit of a perfect body will leave you miserable. Warning: you will never actually lose enough weight to feel satisfied. Warning: the compliments you receive from others can fuel an addiction.

And yet, all of these things are real threats to those who engage in diet culture's demands.

Through the damage I did to my body during my obsession with 'health', I have come to understand, first hand, that we can push our bodies to breaking point in an attempt to attain the ultimate physical form. And, equally as importantly, mental health should never be overlooked in the pursuit of wellness. This is something too many people have learned the hard way.

The issue is that health is too often taken at face value. We only address the issues we can see. If you were to break your leg, it would be plain to see what was wrong. You'd know you were in pain. You'd acknowledge your suffering. But when you are struggling mentally, not only is it very hard to reach out for support, but you often don't even realize you are suffering with something yourself until it's gone too far.

Neglecting the signals that your brain and body send leads to a total distrust between the two and can cause you to become unwell in the long run.

In reaching breaking point mentally, you can also wreak havoc with your body's functions. We cannot ignore the link between the brain and the body. When a person is suffering with their mental health, the physical impacts are not limited to, but can include: headaches, stomach aches, back pain, ulcers, fatigue, digestive issues and a weakened immune system. If you're wondering why you're getting ill a lot, or have headaches that seem to have no cause, start by asking yourself: when was the last time I felt genuinely relaxed? We cannot have good physical health if our mental health is suffering. Anxiety and stress have so many physical effects on the body – not limited to raised heart rate and higher blood pressure. Putting yourself through added stress and anxiety to attain the picture-perfect ideal of 'health' is actually incredibly counterintuitive, and can do more harm than good.

Planned relaxation

For some people, relaxing can be challenging. As a neurodivergent person, my capacity for relaxation is small, although I know how much it benefits me. I can tell when I have managed to relax because I feel refreshed and ready to tackle life, and I find myself wondering why I don't make time to chill out more often. The thing is, when you live with productivity guilt, simply doing a relaxing activity doesn't necessarily mean your body and mind will calm down. Even when you're trying to do something nice for yourself, your brain may be stuck on thoughts like, *I could be using this time productively*, or *There's so much I need to do.*

This is where planned relaxation helps. You don't need to 'rest productively', and this is not to put pressure on achieving tranquillity. Truthfully, if every five minutes you ask yourself, *am I relaxed yet?*, you probably won't be. I'm calling it planned relaxation, but don't tell yourself that you're trying to relax, just think of this as time to do something you enjoy. If you come out of it feeling rejuvenated, that's a bonus.

I want you to plan a dedicated morning/afternoon/evening/entire day in which you are only going to do activities that you find soothing. I understand that life is busy and finding time is tough, but you are really important, and this matters.

At the centre of a mind map, or as a heading of a list, write: *What helps me to wind down?*

Ideas for relaxing activities:
- Gratitude journaling
- Reading
- Painting
- Yoga
- Jewellery making
- Getting your nails done
- Arts and crafts
- A pottery or painting class
- A bubble bath
- A walk in your favourite place
- A pamper shower
- Watching a comfort film
- Baking
- Phone-free time with a friend
- Getting a massage
- Making a flower arrangement
- Watching TV

Choose one, two or three of the above activities that you feel could fit within your allotted relaxation time. These need to be pressure-free, so know that you can spend as much or as little time on each of your chosen activities, and if you don't manage to do all that you chose, that is totally okay! This is time for you, not for your perfectionism.

> I hope you will feel the benefit of taking time for yourself, and please know you deserve to do so regularly. Whether it's one day a week or one day a month, scheduled time where you're not *supposed* to be doing anything may be really beneficial.

The productivity culture and obsessiveness around regular workouts can also damage our bodies. You are so much more likely to be burnt out, run down and in turn catch a cold or get a viral illness when your brain is totally exhausted, as your body will be too, and it won't be able to fight for itself in the ways it needs to. When you ignore the signals your body sends you, or brush them off as 'laziness' or lack of motivation, you leave yourself prone to injury.

Effectively, if you don't allow your body to rest, it will force you to. You will burn it out and you will find yourself injured or unwell.

Fundamental health is looking after your mind, body and soul and rewriting what looking after your body means. Too many people have understood 'look after your body' to mean restriction and punishment, and as a result we are left with a society that doesn't know how to rest without guilt, or how to find enjoyment in exercise. Looking after your body is resting when you are tired, eating when you're hungry, sleeping a full 8–10 hours even if that means you have less time awake to do 'productive' things, eating in abundance and not restricting the range of food groups your body needs.

Fundamental health is the knowledge that a person's weight, size or body shape cannot tell you if they are truly healthy or not. Besides, within society, and unfortunately within the health system, there is so much weight stigma. Instagram comments are full of fatphobia and body shaming. Fat, though a totally neutral word, is still taken as an insult. The truth is, you absolutely cannot tell if a person is healthy or not by the way they look. I remember my friend, when she was physically extremely unwell with an eating disorder, was told by a nurse that she was 'so jealous of her figure'. Regardless of the fact that's an extremely unprofessional thing to say, it also just highlights how nonsensical it is to equate a person's body with their health. My friend was hospitalized for a deadly eating disorder. Getting her body to that point nearly killed her. The correlation between health and body size just isn't there in the way we think it is.

I currently do the least-rigid exercise programme I have ever done and my body is the healthiest and my mind the happiest they have ever been. As we discussed at the outset of this journey, healing your self-talk begins with listening to yourself. And when you listen to yourself, you'll discover both what brings you joy and what brings you down, and, often, that you've been putting unfair pressure on yourself.

I hope you have seen how self-imposed rules only limit your life. You can rest whenever you want, eat what you enjoy, run if you love it, or skip it if you don't. You can embrace your body exactly as it is, give yourself a hug, move when you want to, get cosy when you don't – this is *your* life. Find what makes you feel truly healthy and happy, and know that it's good enough.

Health looks different on everybody.

Chapter 13
Maintain

Healing isn't linear.

As a person who finds comfort in predictability, coping with the non-linear nature of healing has been a task in itself. When I set out on my own healing journey, the discomfort I felt largely stemmed from the unfamiliarity of it all. Self-hatred felt safe. I knew what I was doing and I did it well. That is the reason I stayed so entrenched in toxic patterns of behaviour for so long. If I was critiquing myself, I felt protected. Self-acceptance sounded great but far off; however, once I'd made the decision to actively work on my self-talk, I was hopeful that I'd feel just as comforted if I was able to embrace myself.

But the grey area that was the healing process felt so turbulent to me, so uncertain. I was taking huge strides forward and being humbled as I tripped back into behaviours I longed to be free from. Nothing was definite and predictable, and that filled me with anxiety. It was in those moments that I had to choose to be the strongest I could be, to resist the urge to go all or nothing and dive deep into the habits I was building a life away from. In many ways, and I felt this especially in recovery from my mental health struggles, maintaining the progress you have made is the hardest part of the journey. When you are a person prone to slipping into destructive behaviours, you can't take your eye off the ball for too long. That doesn't mean you will forever be in a battle with yourself – it will absolutely become easier, the thoughts quieter – but you may also be vulnerable to falling back into negative self-talk. It is so important to notice the early warning signs, which we will cover in this chapter.

Even now, despite wholly accepting myself, when life is particularly stressful my brain can throw curveballs. Recently, during the most turbulent time of my life to date, I found myself struggling to complete my basic daily tasks. My brain felt so full I couldn't comprehend tackling my work. I couldn't think straight and everything felt jumbled. I was okay with it for a little while, but as life piled more and more onto my plate, I started to feel like I was sinking. I broke up with my long-term boyfriend, moved out of the flat I'd grown to feel at home in, my dad was critically unwell and I'd lost two people I loved in a short span of time. Instead of being gentle with myself as I'd learned to, and saying, *hey, it's okay that you're struggling! Your whole life is falling apart!*, I noticed that I had started to tell myself that I was failing.

Thoughts of how useless I was and how I was just not built for life crept back into my peripheral. I had started to compare myself again to people I followed online, who also had turbulent lives but still managed to do more than I was able to. The ability to give myself grace seemed to have slipped from my grasp and I was so upset. Panicked, I remember thinking to myself: *I thought I had healed from this. I thought I had moved past this.* I was writing a book about being kind to yourself, what a fraud I was to be thinking so unsympathetically of myself. Becoming aware of my thoughts only intensified the feeling of failure I was already experiencing – it seemed I'd even failed at the thing I'd worked hardest on over the past few years – being gentle, understanding and compassionate to myself.

After some conversations with close friends, gentle reassurance from loved ones, as well as many (unfiltered) journal entries, I remembered to listen, myself, to the advice that I gave so many others. Taking a step back doesn't mean you're at square one again, it just means you're struggling right now. And struggling with something you thought you'd healed from doesn't mean you've failed. You're not in the place you were. Things won't be how they used to be. You're being presented with an opportunity to show yourself kindness in the face of extreme difficulty.

And I knew that was true. No way was I in the place I once had been. I like to appreciate the small wins in every scenario, but the huge win here was not only how quickly I'd noticed I was being unkind to myself but more how unhappy I was with that habit. I no longer felt safe and comfortable in self-hatred, I felt upset and let down by allowing myself to beat myself up in that way. That was, paradoxically, a wonderful thing.

When you have reached a place where you no longer engage in self-criticism in the way you once did, the fear of slipping back and of losing all your progress often becomes prominent. You may become hyper-aware of the possibility that even after all your hard work you could become the unhappier, unkinder version of yourself again. The fear of slipping back can feel quite paralysing, especially when we do not understand that, as humans, a level of negative self-talk is normal. That isn't to say you deserve to speak to yourself unkindly, it just means that human brains are wired in a way which means all of us, at some point, will criticize ourselves in ways others wouldn't.

You haven't failed because you had a self-critical thought. You haven't undone all of your progress because you find yourself in a negative thought spiral. You are going to struggle. You are going to be sad at points in life. But those times are an opportunity to continue to grow, and to prove how strong your relationship with yourself is, and how much you value your own happiness.

Focus on the fact you can notice a difference in your thought patterns. At one point this was your normal. There was a time in your life where you didn't question the fact that you spoke to yourself in this way. Now you can not only notice those thoughts but acknowledge the issue with them. That is a *huge* win. Blips are a totally normal part of the non-linear nature of healing. Don't let the blip itself become a reason to be critical or unkind to yourself.

Grounding

One grounding technique I used while going through trauma therapy, which I feel is quite transferable to this situation, is to list the differences between my life now and my life back then.

I used this to help bring my awareness back to the present day and to remind the part of my brain stuck in the past that we were okay now; we were in a different place, a different year, a different life.

This may be helpful when you feel panicked at the prospect of relapsing into old patterns and mindsets. What is different now? What in your life has changed? Can you think of 3, 5, 10 things you like about yourself? Could you have done that before you started this journey?

You are not the same person as you were yesterday, or a week ago, or a month ago. You have made steps forward that you once didn't believe were possible to take. You have learned too much to ever be the self-hateful, scared person you once were. You are doing just fine.

The likelihood is that you will continue to feel sad at times, and you will face struggles, but sadness doesn't mean things are 'bad' again. It may feel scary to find yourself struggling again when you've been doing well for a while, but sadness is a natural, human part of life, and as long as you aren't being unkind to yourself because of it, you don't need to fear it.

It's important to keep your thoughts and mental discourse around slip-ups neutral. When you get angry at yourself and you decide you've failed or messed up, you are opening the door to a further negative spiral. Noticing you have tripped up a little is your chance to stop negative self-talk in its tracks and to practise what you have learned: to be kind to yourself in the face of adversity. Reframe the negative thoughts you are having about yourself, just as you practised in Chapter 7 (page 121). Hopefully, as we near the final stages of this journey, you will find it much easier to not just flip those thoughts, but to bring in positive self-talk and speak kindly about yourself.

Key reminders as you move through life as a sensitive soul

As a sensitive soul, I have accepted, albeit grudgingly, that I will always be prone to overthinking. I feel things deeply. I am wired to experience emotions intensely, and worrying unnecessarily about things I do not need to comes hand in hand with that. No matter how much work I do, I will always need to stay one step ahead of my anxious brain.

One thing that I've had to tackle head-on is the unyielding fear that I have upset people in my life. I can quickly become paralysed by a fear that they are angry and upset with me because I have picked up on a vibe that isn't actually there, but that I worry is evidence they don't like me. Though I cope so much better with these thoughts now, to a point where I can talk myself out of them, they still come up.

If you, like me, are a sensitive soul, these reminders may prove helpful for you.

The adults you have friendships or relationships with can tell you if something is wrong

You do not need to second-guess and monitor everyone's emotions. You don't need to be on hyper alert, attuned to any small change in the vibe. People can tell you if something has bothered them, or if you've done something wrong. It is not your responsibility to panic or worry or try to read into what 'could be' small signals. Don't torture yourself, convincing yourself that others hate you, when there is no concrete evidence to support that – anxious brains can make us believe we are seeing signs that really aren't there.

If you can step back from a situation, rationalize your anxiety and there is *still* evidence that somebody is acting differently with you, it doesn't automatically mean you've done something wrong but even if there is, there is nothing you can do about it unless you are aware, or are made aware of what you have done wrong. As adults, when something upsets us it's our responsibility to bring it up and talk it out. It is terrible for your nervous system to be around people who make you second-guess whether they like you or not, and healthy communication is key in friendships and relationships. Until you are told something is wrong, assume nothing is wrong, or you will spend your precious time in a state of avoidable anxiety.

Your body is naturally going to change

Bodies change. At 25, you will not look the same as when you were 16, and at 30, you will not look the same as you will when you are 40. You are not meant to. You are supposed to grow and change. Your body is supposed to get bigger in places, it may shift the way it holds fat, and your bone structure may even change, too. As our lives change and adapt, so do our bodies.

Embrace it all, with kindness and compassion for your body. This body is the only one you will have in this life. It deserves your respect and kindness. Do not let the changes you will go through, no matter what, keep you from speaking to yourself with the care and understanding that you deserve.

What a privilege it is to age, and how incredible that our bodies are so resilient and resourceful. Ageing is a process to be thankful for, not ashamed of.

Your emotions serve a purpose

Please refrain from beating yourself up for the fact that you are a sensitive soul. Not everyone in this world is going to understand your emotions and reactions to things, but that doesn't mean that what you think and feel is wrong. Even years into your healing journey, when you think you have got a solid grip on your self-talk, you may be thrown curveballs and thoughts will come in that don't align with the way you know you want to talk to yourself. Again, they are not stupid or irrelevant thoughts. You feel the things you feel for a reason, your brain and body don't attach emotion to things out of nowhere. You are not silly. You may feel things more deeply than others but that can also be a blessing. The beauty of being a deep-feeler is that you can experience joy in such an intricate way. As a person who feels their feelings, all of my emotions seem to pulse through my veins. There is nothing low-key about the way I feel. And though sometimes exhausting, it is such a blessing to feel so deeply. You are likely more empathetic, understanding and kind because you have spent so much time in your own mind. Thoughts that come up for you, even after you believed you had healed from their root cause, are not a sign of your own weakness.

Though we focus a lot on overcoming the root cause of our struggles, there is great importance in tolerating hardship and allowing ourselves to feel difficult emotions. One of the most challenging parts of my healing journey was actually learning to ride the wave of emotion. Sitting with emotions was never something I found easy by any means; I was perpetually overwhelmed, and when the worst of my feelings hit, I felt desperate to just switch my brain off, to run away from it all. I used to cope with what I felt by literally doing anything *but* feeling. So, I understand as much as anyone how it feels to want to escape your brain.

As much as I'd love to say that ignorance was bliss, it never was. The intensity of the emotions I felt only grew when they were ignored. Through every small act of self-rejection – telling myself I was overreacting, trying to distract myself constantly, saying I was fine when I was far from it – the pressure grew. Dismissed emotion would swell inside me until I'd reached the moment I'd burst, and I'd be forced to face all of the feelings I'd been ignoring. That was an incredibly unhealthy cycle for me, as feeling it all took me to very dark places and led me into impulsive and damaging ways of coping.

I found that although sitting with emotion was extremely painful in the short term, it was helping me. In fact, the more I sat with my emotions and let myself feel, the more capable I felt and the easier it was to show myself that I was strong, and I was able to survive whatever my mind threw at me. Learning to tolerate difficult feelings helped me build my sense of strength and my confidence in the fact that even if I did struggle in the future, I could experience the worst and be okay. Where I used to periodically be struck down by big buildups and extreme outbursts, I was slowly learning how to hold myself and acknowledge my needs. I was giving myself a hug, sometimes literally, and saying, 'this is really hard right now'. That was what I had needed for so long, but I couldn't show up for myself in that way because I was so full of self-hatred. I couldn't seek comfort from myself when I was my biggest bully.

The beauty of this life is that even when nobody else does, you can always show up for yourself. You are the one person who can always be in your corner.

Through the process of learning to ride the wave and sit with hard feelings, I had more space to acknowledge what had triggered me in the first place. I now find that when feelings come up that in the past I'd have tried to ignore, I can put my arms around myself and say, 'you're finding things really hard right now and that's okay'. And then, when I feel calmer, I can ask myself 'what is making things feel so hard right now?'

Sometimes the act of healing your self-talk isn't so rational and adult. Sometimes it's just becoming a friend to yourself, but sometimes it's talking to yourself as if you're a toddler, or as if you're parenting yourself. When you've lived so much of your life not really being in touch with your emotions or understanding yourself, you can end up dysregulated. Remember that you are a human, still figuring things out, and going back to basics – speaking to yourself in gentle, simple terms can be really helpful. In moments when I am engulfed by huge emotions, my brain can feel a little like a toddler throwing a tantrum. It just screams and screams in overwhelm, and nothing seems to help. By being gentle and comforting, hearing myself and acknowledging myself, I can begin to comfort and calm that bit of my mind.

A difficult, but very effective, question that I have taken to asking myself in emotional moments is: 'something about this situation is making things feel hard, I wonder if this resonates with something I've felt in the past?'

Gently digging, not in a way that holds any shame or suggests fault, to try to understand the trigger for your feeling has taught me a lot about myself, now and the past versions of me.

It may also be helpful for you to identify your triggers, so that when certain feelings come up for you in the future, you can quickly understand what has caused this feeling to arise.

Thought spirals

I remember during one of the first conversations I had with a therapist, I was introduced to the pink elephant phenomenon. It revolutionized the way I saw unwanted or intrusive thoughts and feelings.

'Close your eyes,' he said. I obediently closed my eyes. 'Now, I want you to NOT think of a pink elephant. You can think of anything, just don't think about a pink elephant.'

Before you continue reading, I want you to close your eyes and try your hardest, for the next 30 seconds, to <u>not</u> think of a pink elephant.

Behind my eyelids, all that I saw were pink elephants. I kept trying to force them out with other animals I could conjure up images of, desperate to not visualize the forbidden pink elephant. But, no matter what I tried, the pink elephants taunted me. I couldn't make them leave.

At first, it seems like a strange thing to be asked to do in therapy. You might be questioning the relevance of this, but the pink elephant taught me one of the most important lessons I've learned. It taught me that the harder you try to not think about something, the more you will think about it. And the more you try to suppress your feelings, the harder it will become to ignore them. Albeit a difficult truth, the best way to deal with emotions is to *feel* emotions.

When you have a moment, grab a piece of paper, open your Notes app or find some space in your journal. Can you pinpoint any feelings that come up for you often which you feel the urge to avoid? Can you think of any emotions that you push away rather than facing?

What are they? Write a few sentences about how they show up for you, and how they make you feel in yourself. Do they trigger certain thought spirals? If so, what sort of thoughts accompany these feelings? Can you spot a pattern in the times when these thoughts usually show up for you?

Facing painful thoughts and feelings is understandably an unpleasant activity. When you stifle what you don't want to feel, however, it will quickly become a pink elephant. So, you face a choice – create a safe space for yourself in which you can process what you're dealing with, or continue to be ambushed by unpleasant emotions and feelings.

Maintaining the progress you have made also involves accepting that the progress you have made may not always feel like a linear, upward trajectory. When, after months of fostering a really wholesome and healthy relationship with yourself, the little negative voice is chirping in your ear again, your progress has not been undone. There are parts of our minds and our lives that we cannot control and there is a level of negative self-talk that is a natural part of life in some ways. It is going to come in, and it is going to invite you to spiral down into self-hateful thoughts.

The maintenance phase is about standing your ground. Remembering all that you have learned about yourself. Focusing on the good. The good in you and the good in your life that has become more apparent since you shifted your focus outwards. There is too much good that comes from self-acceptance to go back into a self-critical place. Though it can feel comforting, that false pretence of comfort will slowly wear you down. Stand strong in your kindness.

No matter what happens, no matter what your brain throws at you, you are worthy of self-acceptance. You deserve a life free of self-hatred. You deserve to spend your time focused on positive, joyful things. You deserve to make memories and to be in the photos of them. You deserve more than to hide away. You deserve light and love. You deserve life.

Chapter 14

Protect

Find the strength inside you to set the boundaries you deserve.

The more respect I had for myself, the more I valued my own happiness, the easier it was to spot when I was spending time with somebody who was bringing me down. I have always been a very self-aware person, perhaps to a fault, but what I became aware of during the later phases of my healing was that I was, without doubt, a people-pleaser.

My tendency to prioritize the needs of others over my own left me in situations I didn't want to be in, overstimulated and uncomfortable, anxious and trapped. I didn't have to live this way but I chose others' comfort over mine. I would sooner sit with my own discomfort than say no to what others asked of me, and so I ended up doing things I truly didn't want to do.

This went hand in hand with my inability to speak up for myself and my desperation to be liked. As most psychological phenomena do, my people-pleasing tendencies hadn't stemmed from nowhere. This behaviour, though, the fear of saying no, was deeply rooted in my worries around being disliked, of being ostracized. I learned at a young age to copy others' behaviour and try to fit in. I developed an inferiority complex, another thing that switching up my self-talk highlighted to me. I put myself way below everyone else, no matter who they were. I thought everyone was cooler, kinder, prettier, funnier or more popular than me. It didn't matter who they were, I was desperate for them to like me.

Throughout my life, this desperation has tripped me up. It wasn't until recently that I made peace with the fact that not everybody in life is going to like me, and that's okay. I spent years fighting for people to like *me*, when I couldn't really pinpoint any qualities about them that I liked. I viewed myself so negatively that I felt entirely below others, as if I'd be lucky to have friends at all.

Protecting myself from falling back into risky habits, putting the measures in place to avoid slipping back into negative self-talk, means eliminating my people-pleasing. This, to be honest, is something I'm still working on. I'm not ashamed to admit that I still have an urge to people-please in social situations. It's not something you can turn off, especially when it started at a young age.

The concept of not being a people pleaser can feel intimidating when you've used people-pleasing to cope for a long time. It doesn't mean you're going to become a social outcast, hated by all, incapable of being kind. It just means you're going to nurture yourself and value your own needs, even if that means saying no to others. Moving past people-pleasing isn't being mean, it's realizing that you can't put others' happiness before your own, that you can be both kind and in control of your own life. You don't have to bend over backwards for others at your own expense anymore. It is not selfish to remove yourself from situations that harm you.

You may need to cut people off. This is a harsh statement, especially if you're terrified of conflict. Imagining arguments and hurting people's feelings is unpleasant, but it doesn't have to be big and scary and it may even happen naturally; if you end up giving less of your energy to a friendship you may come to realize that, actually, you were the one putting in all of the effort. When you stop pouring energy into something that isn't valued by the other person, it may fizzle out. It's okay if it hurts, it can be incredibly painful to realize a relationship is one-sided. Just know that you deserve to be valued, cherished and cared for. You deserve more than to feel as though you are carrying a friendship.

Protecting your progress, protecting your peace, protecting your own needs and happiness – all of these are so important in the journey to self-acceptance. To find true happiness within, true contentment within yourself, you must cover all areas.

Self-acceptance isn't just about your body or your appearance, it's also the realization that you deserve better than how you are being treated. To tolerate that self-acceptance itself isn't a linear journey. The understanding that some people may not like you and that it isn't a fault of your own. The acceptance that you're not going to be everyone's person but that doesn't signify a fault within you. The knowledge that you will make mistakes and have regrets. And the recognition that it doesn't make you a bad person.

Priorities for protecting your progress

Staying consistent with the practices you have learned in this book are vital in keeping the dialogue positive or neutral. There are, however, checkpoints for things you need to stay on top of and keep an eye on periodically throughout your life.

Noticing when your thoughts are becoming negative

We have covered self-connection and recognizing negative and unhelpful thoughts when they come in both Part 2 (page 73) and the previous chapter (page 201), but protecting yourself also involves being one step ahead. There may be times that your thoughts have slipped a little and you haven't noticed. It's good to check in, perhaps through journal prompts at the end of each month, or any other way that works for you.

Throughout this journey you will have gained a greater understanding of your own emotions and perhaps a greater awareness of your own unhappiness. If your thoughts do start to have a negative tinge to them, it's time to look at the life factors impacting you. Are you feeling fulfilled at work? Have you been facing any major stressors? What is your body image like right now? What do you feel when you look in the mirror? Are there any relationships that feel draining? Is there anybody in your life you're dreading seeing?

Once you are aware of factors impacting your unhappiness, you can form an action plan to tackle them head on. As is life, there may be things that are out of your control yet are still impacting your self-talk. If you cannot tackle the contributing factors, shift your focus to your self-care practices. Make sure you're allocating time for yourself and the things that make you feel good. Be strict with yourself, even if it means saying no to people so you can have an evening to look after yourself. Routinely journal and include positive affirmations, reminding yourself of all of the good within you. Make a conscious effort to be kind to yourself.

Not tolerating behaviour from others that makes you feel small

The premise of not being a people-pleaser is to not tolerate things that make you uncomfortable for the sake of somebody else. If you know you are a people-pleaser, or have a tendency to stay in relationships for the benefit of others, it could be helpful to you to take a mindful moment after seeing somebody. Take a moment to notice how your energy levels feel and how tense or not you are. When checking in with yourself, if you become aware of a feeling of dread or fatigue before or after seeing somebody, it may be time to dig deeper into why that is.

We all have a different level of social battery. Personally, I get tired pretty quickly if I don't feel totally comfortable around somebody. It'll be clear to me quite quickly that I don't, because I'll be dreading the next time I have to be with them.

I am very in-tune with my feelings, but not everybody finds it easy to be, so here are some signs to spot that may show you're in a friendship or relationship that is doing you more harm than good:

- You come away feeling tired.
- You want to withdraw socially.
- You feel more anxious around them.
- The idea of seeing them again doesn't feel exciting to you.
- They are critical or judgemental of you.
- You replay things they said to you that didn't sit right with you.
- They enjoy talking badly about others behind their backs/are often negative.
- You find yourself overthinking what you're saying while with them.

You don't have to force yourself to stay friends with somebody if it's draining you. Other people's emotions are not your responsibility and you owe it to yourself to protect your own happiness. It's not selfish to step back from a relationship that leaves you feeling worse.

Staying connected to yourself and your true needs

Though in a similar vein to checking in with yourself, this is more about developing, or strengthening, your ability to say no to things. To avoid burnout, or being socially drained, you may have to say no to people sometimes. Perhaps it's my British-ness, but saying 'no' has always felt rude to me, and it is something I still struggle to do with confidence sometimes. It has never been very comfortable for me to turn down invitations, and I worry about offending people. I know, however, that I feel that way because of the people-pleasing instinct I carry.

It is not rude or ungrateful to need a day off. It's not unkind to want to be alone for a day rather than agree to plans you're not feeling up to.

Removing people or situations from your life that negatively impact you

As mentioned before, this doesn't have to be as harsh as it sounds. Guilt around what will happen if you distance yourself from a friend can keep you in friendships that feel like a chore. The truth is, you're allowed to just not want to see people anymore. Everyone grows and changes; sometimes you will just outgrow people.

I have a few friends who are extremely brave in this aspect, friends who will, albeit gently, tell people if they don't want to hang out anymore and will give them a reason. Though I've never been as upfront as them, I have learnt a lot from them about not giving my time to those who do not value it, or who don't make me feel uplifted and energized when we're finished hanging out.

The both wonderful and upsetting reality is that people in your life, as time goes on, are going to change. Change is one of the only certain parts of life. And in the same way that people in your life now might have changed – you too will grow and develop, with age and with experiences that will shape and alter you. Your opinions, interests and hobbies may shift, and with that, you may be a different person to who you once were.

Naturally, when people change, relationships change. In my personal experience, especially as a person who hates change, this has been a fact I've found hard to face. You will drift from friends you were once extremely close to, and you will find close friends in people you'd have clashed with in the past. Sometimes the person you once felt closest to in the world becomes somebody you no longer click with, and slowly you notice the time you spend with them feels more and more draining. It can feel so scary to slip away from somebody you had such a close bond with, and although I definitely encourage leaving relationships that make you unhappy, struggles don't necessarily have to end friendships. There is value in communication and in making an attempt to find your way back to what you once had; perhaps openly talking things through would highlight areas for both people to work on.

Besides, when friends grow into a person you no longer find comfort and companionship in, that doesn't mean you'll never be compatible again. Though we didn't fall out, at age 11, my childhood best friend and I drifted apart after nine years of friendship. We were both growing into our teenage personalities, and for two years we didn't really talk. As had been my experience of friendship throughout school, I assumed that the end was always the end.

But we found our way back to each other a few years later. We had both grown in different directions, and then we grew back together again. We've been best friends for over 21 years, and I'm so grateful we came back together, because nobody has been by my side like Beth.

Some relationships will stand the test of time and will grow in ways that mean both parties are still compatible, but some simply won't. Despite knowing that somebody is so clearly unhelpful for you to be friends with, it can still be difficult to let people go. There is a temptation to cling to the memory of who they were, to keep giving them the benefit of the doubt and hoping the person you found friendship or love within is still there. When you refuse to let that hope go, though, you will drain yourself by staying in situations with somebody who is not good for you.

Dig deep. Find the strength inside you to set the boundaries you deserve. Friendships and relationships can be boundaried and still have the wonderful, comforting feeling that the best friendships have. I'm certain a lot of people will struggle with the concept of setting boundaries. After all, how do you go about it? It's not something we're taught, though arguably it should be.

It sounds formal, but it really doesn't need to be. You don't need to send out a mass email to everybody in your life, bullet-pointing each of your boundaries. It can be as simple as saying, 'Sorry, I keep Sundays free so that I have a day to myself' when arranging a plan. Or, 'I'm going to be tired after a social event that day, so I'd rather not do that evening'. That is setting a boundary. Making time for yourself or saying no to something for your own good is not selfish. Another example of setting a boundary could be, 'I really don't feel comfortable talking about this subject, please can we avoid it?'

A boundary is not a big scary fence, built to block people out and make things awkward. Think of boundaries as creating paths to make the route less confusing and easier to follow, so nobody goes off track and ends up hurt. Setting boundaries is drawing a line around your land and not letting anybody trample on the flowers you're trying to grow. It's reclaiming your power and your personal space, and it's a hugely important part of self-respect.

People who deserve to be in your life will acknowledge and respect your boundaries. Good friends will want the best for you. If people struggle with your boundaries, it may be a sign that they don't value your needs. Yes, it's important to be compassionate, but it's equally important to prioritize your own wellbeing, and sometimes letting go of people who don't respect your boundaries is the kindest thing you can do for yourself.

Protecting the progress you have made requires putting yourself first, even when it feels uncomfortable. You can be a good person and set boundaries. You can be a kind person and disagree with others. You can be a caring person and say no to people. It isn't selfish to respect your own needs and wants.

Chapter 15
Who Are You?

*It's time to reclaim yourself.
It's time to get to know
the true you.*

Five years ago, I was terrified at the prospect of knowing myself. All I'd ever known was what I *wasn't* – I wasn't funny, I wasn't cool, I wasn't popular – and I'd settled for a life revolving around self-punishment. Having spent such a large portion of my life believing there was nothing to me, I'd jump for joy seeing the person I am today.

I am confident in myself. I am a good listener. I am kind and I care deeply about the people in my life. I enjoy things – yoga, dog walks, creating, coffee with friends, reading, board games, mindless TV – and that in itself is so significant. When I was consumed by negative self-talk, I didn't have the mental energy to find pleasure in activities. But I enjoy things now. I love to help people. I adore animals. I don't hide my excitement when I meet dogs in cafés. I have a great sense of humour. It is easy to list the things I like about myself. I've never felt more like me, and to think this is a feeling I once feared is unimaginable now.

I know now that to admit this doesn't mean I'm cocky. I know now that holding a positive opinion of myself isn't arrogance. It's self-confidence, which I deserve to feel. I feel no shame in sitting here and writing what I like about myself. I worked hard to believe it, so of course I'm going to celebrate it.

If you'd asked me who I was before I started my journey to self-acceptance, I'd have thrown a hundred insulting adjectives your way before I'd have managed to tell you one good thing about myself. The view I held of myself was very short-sighted. My worth was measured in 'what' I was. I never paid attention to the 'whys', or 'hows', or 'whos' that made me, me.

Through building my self-confidence I have found I've become much more interested in not just the world around me, but in what makes me, me, because when I engage in what truly makes me happy, I am fulfilled.

This journey has been one of getting to know myself after feeling lost for so long, and I have come out of it with an understanding of my 'whys' – why I do what I do, why I care about what I care about, why I sometimes take things more personally than others, why that doesn't show weakness. It's enabled me to see the value in, and to get better at, my 'hows' – how to show up for the people in my life, how to make change in society, how to look after myself when things feel difficult, how to nurture all the versions of myself who live within me and who will in the future. And, because we are so influenced by the people we choose to have in our lives, it has also meant being more intentional with my 'whos' – who do I give my time to, who makes me feel like the best version of myself?

This is who I am. I have learned that I am not a list of adjectives. I am not my opinions on my body, or hair, or appearance, or personality. Who I am is what I offer to the world, how I treat others and myself. I am multifaceted and complex, and to summarize my entire being into a few words as I used to isn't possible. We are all made up of our 'whys', 'hows' and 'whos', and life becomes richer and more fulfilling when that is your focus, not the superficial, limiting world of labelling 'what' you are.

It's time to reclaim yourself. It's time to get to know the true you. Who are you? It doesn't have to be an overwhelming question, it can be exciting – you will forever be growing and changing and discovering new parts of yourself that make you, *you*.

As you progress through this journey, I hope you find connection with yourself in a way you haven't before. You no longer need to be at war with yourself. You owe it to yourself to be open and compassionate to all versions of you. The energy it takes from you to be on a constant quest to fix yourself is huge. That energy you gave to perfectionism without realizing can be redirected for good, to learn about yourself and what you really care about. Away from societal pressure, expectations, beauty standards and misplaced priorities, who are you?

Changing the way you talk to yourself will, inevitably, change your behaviour. Hopefully you will feel less of a need to put on a front to the world and can become comfortable being your unfiltered self. This is a process of unmasking. Although unmasking is a term often used around neurodivergence, anybody who has lived with an inner critic has likely been living with shame. And, as a result, your unreserved, authentic self may have been buried deep inside. There will be a level of unmasking as you come to accept yourself. It may feel like being out of control at points, no longer putting immense pressure on yourself to be a certain way, but embracing *you* is an energy-giver like no other.

In taking off the mask, you will build confidence in the fact that you are likeable, you are fun to be around, you don't have to be squished into a mould you don't fit into in order to be liked by others. You will see that who you are is enough. Because it is. You are enough. Funny enough, cool enough, pretty enough, clever enough – you are enough as you are.

In the past year I have really felt myself unmask, not just around those I am most comfortable with but with new people I meet. I now enter social situations with much more confidence and with a knowledge that actually being my true, unfiltered self is a good thing. I am often very honest and don't keep much about myself secret, which used to embarrass me. I felt like my anxiety caused me to word-vomit and I'd end up pre-emptively worrying about what was going to come out of my mouth. But I've realized that actually makes people feel more comfortable around me. When I enter situations with no pretence, no desperation to impress, others feel more at ease to be themselves too. I've started to look at my anxious waffling with a 'who cares' perspective. We all take ourselves too seriously. Let's all be a little more human, silly and awkward – and be okay with it.

Actually, the more I have got to know myself, the less rigid I've become. I still don't like change – that is a feature I came built-in with, I think – but I am now much more open to taking in new information and understanding others' perspectives. As is the nature of being alive on a fast-moving and ever-changing planet, I am constantly observing and absorbing what happens in the world around me, as well as online. That will, inescapably, be impacting and affecting the beliefs I hold and my understanding of the world, but it feels less intimidating to me now that I am confident in who I am. Change feels a little more okay because I know what I value – kindness, understanding, equality, respect – and those values provide a constant for me. Being a constant for myself in an age that is so overwhelming, with so much information being fed to me from all angles, bombarded by stimuli, is so important.

I used to feel a little like a house of cards, and any sign of bad weather would knock me right down. My rigidity made me delicate, vulnerable. Now I feel more like a skyscraper, storms will come but I have built myself to sway in the wind. I am sure and strong, and being self-assured allows me to adapt.

Connecting with who you are also involves being open to vulnerability and approaching all of your emotions without judgement. As we discussed in Part 3, there are no good or bad thoughts, just thoughts. It's what we do with them that matters. Who you are is deeply rooted in your intentions. Sometimes you will have thoughts that may feel unkind or harsh. Remember not to view every thought as a reflection of who you are, or your values. Your thoughts, especially the first ones you have about things, are often voiced by influences throughout your life, in wider society, your family or relationships. They don't necessarily reflect your beliefs. Who you are lies in how you feel about the thoughts you have had, not the thought itself.

Q&A with yourself

If you are struggling to know who you are, or to connect with what makes you, you, try asking yourself these questions:

- How do I show up for myself day to day?
- Why do I feel it's important to talk to myself with kindness?
- How do I make others' lives better?
- Who do I feel the most 'me' when I'm around?
- Why is that?

Sometimes people struggle to know who they are because it's so easy to forget that what defines you isn't the colour of your eyes, the clothes you wear, the music you like or what you do for work. You are what you do for yourself and for others, you are what you believe and what you stand for. You don't have to define yourself at all, in fact. You can just be.

Many people, like me, have felt they are uninteresting, or have nothing to them because they are a person who doesn't have many hobbies. Icebreaker questions were my nemesis because I didn't have a hobby that I do regularly and am dedicated to. For a long time, I thought I was a boring person because I didn't give much time to my interests and passions. When I changed the way I spoke to myself, the knock-on effect was that my life opened up. I grew in confidence and I walked into more scenarios that I'd usually have avoided. I met new people and reconnected with others who I hadn't seen for a long time. I said yes to more invitations, because I no longer felt the perfectionist shame that came with not being good at something on the first try.

When I stopped reducing my entire being into what I was and instead focused on who I was, I found out that actually there were a lot of things I was passionate about. I tried hobbies I'd always wished I was confident enough to try. You're not boring because you don't have a huge group of friends or do loads with your free time, but actually, when you stop telling yourself you're boring, your life may just open up a lot.

You are interesting, and layered, and fun to be around, and you will find enjoyment in things in life that you haven't even discovered yet. Don't lose hope or be down on yourself because you got a little lost along the way. It's never too late to explore your passions, nor to try new things.

Don't be afraid of who you are. Embrace all parts of you, past and present, healing and flawed. There are versions of you that you haven't even met yet, but by being kind to yourself now, when you finally do, you will be the best version of yourself.

If there's one certain first step in getting to know yourself, it is to make time for yourself. Schedule in time to actively take care of yourself. Know that you matter. This is your life, and you are the only person who is going to live it. Give yourself space to learn about *you*. What do *you* care about? What do *you* believe?

There is one person on this Earth who has control over your actions and decisions, and that is you. Opinions of others only hold any weight if we choose to let them. You will never be unjudgeable to anybody because you cannot control others' minds, but you can choose to not let others' judgements infiltrate your self-talk. You can choose to be kind to yourself.

In an ever-changing world, be your constant. Be your rock. Be the person you can always trust to listen to you with an open heart. Be kind to yourself, always.

This is the only body you will ever live in, so let it be your home.

Afterword

With the sun just a sliver now, sinking into the sea, darkness draws in. My feet are quickly becoming numb; even during summer, the water in Ireland is bitterly cold. Leaving footprints beside pawprints in the sand, Bea and I make our way back up the beach. I can't help but think about how lucky I am to have found an animal who shows me such unconditional love.

The wind brushes through the dunes with a sigh. Unwilling to disturb the quiet, though I know we're alone here, I whisper to Bea. 'It's time to go home now.'

The legs that carry me are strong, the arms by my side no longer hidden from the world. My heart is full. And although I am wandering along a beach in Ireland, 500 miles from the house I grew up in, I know that I am home. In a body I spent so long fighting, with a brain I once couldn't bear to live in, I have found a place where I feel safe. The decision to heal is one I will never regret, for as long as I live. When I chose to be kind to myself, I chose to hold life within my palms and say, 'I will not let you break me'. When I chose to make peace with my body and all that has been, I chose to come home. That is what healing is – coming home to yourself.

I know I am safe here. After everything, I am home.

I do not know where life will take me, nor what wonders or challenges await me, but I do know one thing for certain: I am a friend I will never lose. No matter what, I will stand beside myself, and I will hold tightly onto all I have learned. I will take what is thrown my way and I will be okay, because I have myself and that is one thing that I know won't change.

I break into a jog and, not missing a beat, Bea starts running too. The soft sand shifts beneath my feet, and even on solid ground there's no way I could match her pace, so I happily fall behind and watch her bound along the shore. When we're halfway along the beach I stop and let myself breathe, looking out into the ocean to catch one last glimpse of the sun. The sea seems to ebb and flow in time with my breath, I notice, or perhaps I have unintentionally matched its rhythm. Bea turns back, coming to stand beside me, as if questioning why I've stopped. She happily takes off again once I begin to run. Ears flapping in the wind, tail wagging, pawprints overlapping my footprints. The wind stings my eyes but it reminds me that I can breathe. We run and we run. And I have never felt so free.

Acknowledgements

This book wouldn't have been possible without the incredible support system I have around me. It has been a lifelong dream of mine to write and publish a book, and I know my younger self would be in total disbelief (as I am!) that her dream had come true.

Thank you to my incredible editor Cara, Lizzy for commissioning this book and the team at Pan Macmillan. You gave me such strength and encouragement throughout the writing process. I am so lucky to have worked with people who care so much, and who truly value what I stand for.

Thank you to my mum, dad and Rory, who have held me and loved me and who always saw a future for me. I love you all more than you will ever know. And of course, Bea, my soul dog.

Thank you to Sophie and the DDA team for always listening to me, for guiding me and for helping me come into my own.

Thank you to Oscar, who believed in me and made this book possible. I am so grateful to you for your constant support and kindness.

Thank you to all of my friends who have gone above and beyond to be there for me over the years. To Beth, who has been by my side since we were two. To Flora, Jaycie, Kaitlin, Lauren, Amber, Chlo, and many more, you know who you are! I feel truly blessed to be surrounded by such warm, compassionate, beautiful women.

Thank you to my Nana Jess, who has always been a wonderful friend, a cheerleader and a safe space for me. And to all of my family – I love you.

Thank you to Paul Overton, without whom I wouldn't be here today, and who always advocated for what I needed. Thank you to everybody at BPS who went above and beyond for me.

Thank you to the mental health professionals who took care of me when I couldn't take care of myself. And thank you to 2020 me who chose to recover from anorexia. I'm sure most authors don't thank themselves in their acknowledgements, but had I not made that choice, I wouldn't be here writing this. I'm so grateful for life.

Thank you to every person who has ever followed me, left a kind comment, or sent me a sweet message – without the community you have helped me to build online and your endless support, I wouldn't be in the place I am today.

And finally, thank you to *you* for reading this book. Thank you for making a kind decision for yourself, and for wanting to help yourself. You are strong and capable and so deserving of joy. I hope you find it. x